E

in Our Faith

"Once in a while a book comes along that captures our attention, yet rarely one that takes us captive. Annie Paden's book, *Fruit Flies,* does both. Stories from her heart to ours mirror how much alike we really are and gives us a glimpse of the women God intends us to be. You will laugh and you will cry as the Spirit begins to ripen His fruit in your life."

—*Nancy Carlson*
Women's ministry leader, Bible study teacher,
writer, lay counselor and mentor

"I highly recommend this honest, sensitive, humorous, and practical study on the subject of the Fruit of the Spirit. *Fruit Flies* is an essential study for building and/or restoring hope, courage, and faith."

—*Kimberly Davidson, MA*
Board certified through the American Association of Christian Counselors, Kimberly is the author of healing-based women's books including, *Breaking the Cover Girl Mask, I'm Beautiful Why Can't I See It?* and *Dancing in the Sonshine—Restoration from the Wounds of Abuse.*

"One of the best Christian living books I've read. The Fruit of the Spirit in Galatians 5:22-23 come to life as they are fleshed out and presented by the author. Filled with humor, often using her own faux pas to make her points, Annie's gentle encouragement spurs readers to abandon actions that spoil their Christian testimony and instead walk in the Spirit."

—*Julie Surface Johnson*
Author of *Over Coffee* and Christian advice columnist,
Challenges Women Face

Fruit Flies in Our Faith

NURTURING AND SHARING
THE
FRUIT OF THE SPIRIT

Annie Paden

TANGIBLE FAITH PUBLISHING
Gladstone, Oregon

Tangible Faith Publishing
640 Collins Crest
Gladstone, Oregon 97027
www.TangibleFaithPublishing.com

ISBN 978-1-7322403-0-8 soft cover
ISBN 978-1-7322403-1-5 e-book

Cover & interior design: Anita Jones, Another Jones Graphics

Publisher's Cataloging-In-Publication Data
(Prepared by The Donohue Group, Inc.)

Names: Paden, Annie, 1950-
Title: Fruit flies in our faith : nurturing and sharing the fruit of the spirit / Annie Paden.
Description: Gladstone, Oregon : Tangible Faith Publishing, [2018]
Identifiers: ISBN 9781732240308 (paperback) | ISBN 9781732240315 (ebook)
Subjects: LCSH: Paden, Annie--Religion. | Christian life. | Conduct of life.
Classification: LCC BV4501.3 .P34 2018 (print) | LCC BV4501.3 (ebook) | DDC 248.4--dc23

Printed in the Unites States of America

To my husband Rich

Thank you for reading each chapter over and over and over.
Your male perspective always gave me "fresh eyes."
Your encouragement and prayers helped me battle "fruit flies"
and finish what I started.
You are the love of my life. Forty-five years and counting.

Thank You

Julie Johnson – Our friendship, laughter and shared experiences are a gift. You taught me not to be afraid to try something new and to trust God with the results. You believed in me when I was a bit adrift and started me on the adventure of writing. We share so many "do you remember" times. What a deal.

Alice Gray – You once told me if I was going to write not to be afraid of the red pencil. Your experience in editing opened my eyes on how to put together a book so it made sense to the reader. Your red pencil spoke truth with grace. Your kindness and energy rekindled my desire to tell a good story.

Nancy Carlson – You are so talented, painting pictures with words as I never could. And yet you have been my cheerleader since the birth of *Fruit Flies*. God knew I needed a little, red-headed friend whose prayers and determination would keep me going. Now, you finish your book, Nancy. It's a winner!

Kim Davidson – Your knowledge and your ear for what doesn't sound quite right have saved me from awkward writing and out and out blunders. You've taught me to figure out things I don't understand and to persevere even when writing is hard. Your books have opened my eyes and heart to God's healing.

Girlfriends (you know who you are) – My dear Christian sisters, you have shown me what the Fruit of the Spirit looks like in real life. During stressful times or simple day-to-day living you "walk the walk." You demonstrate how to be "real" as you live for Christ. I hope you see yourselves in the pages of *Fruit Flies*. You are all there passing out beautiful fruit.

Susan Patterson – Your encouragement, willingness to share your experience and excellent referrals helped me put the pieces of the puzzle together. The cup of tea and the orange cat on my lap were special touches.

Bev Antonio, Nancy Carlson and Bonnie Marston – Your proofreading skills and "fresh eyes" caught the punctuation and grammatical errors I missed after several read-throughs. Nancy, your Chicago Manual of Style gave me confidence there would be no glaring mistakes in the final copy. You provided the finishing touch to *Fruit Flies*.

Anita Jones – Your creative cover design and interior layout are all I wanted – and then some. You took my pile of pages, thousands of words, and made them into a book. You involved me in the process and your kindness gave me the freedom to accept new ideas and make changes when needed. If I'm ever in Missoula, we're doing lunch. You're wonderful.

Sharon Castlen – Your knowledge and enthusiasm for marketing amaze me. You were patient with my vertical learning curve and "talked me down from the ledge" when I was overwhelmed. You challenged my brain and jettisoned me out of my comfort zone while always providing support and a safety net. God knew I would sit on a box of books forever so He gave me you. Sharon, you are a keeper.

My children and grandchildren – You are a wonderful wealth of stories and are loved more than life itself. I tried hard not to embarrass you in the book. You are all boys so we don't always think and feel the same but that's good. Life is never boring. We are tied together at the heart and nothing can break that bond.

Richie – You are my knight in shining armor, my love, my laughter, and my best friend. Without your encouragement, kindness and sense of humor *Fruit Flies* would never have hatched. You listened, offered constructive advice and let me share stories about you. You will always have my heart.

The *Father* – who loves me so much He sent Jesus and gave me His Word. *Jesus* – who loves me so much He died to save me and gave me His Spirit. The *Holy Spirit* – who loves me so much He fills me with Himself and is teaching me to nurture and share His fruit. You amaze me and fill me with wonder. Thank you.

*But the Fruit of the Spirit is
love, joy, peace,
patience, kindness,
goodness, faithfulness,
gentleness and self-control...*
Galatians 5:22-23

Contents

Introduction

FRUIT FLIES

"Hah!" I smacked the front of my bathrobe. "I got him. The last fruit fly."

"Put on your glasses and check again," my husband, Rich, said.

"He just flew past my nose." Right hand pressed to my chest, I fumbled for my reading glasses. I slowly lifted my fingers and took a look. There it lay.

"I killed a toast crumb," I sighed, dusting off my robe.

"Good effort," Rich said. "Leave him alone. He can't live forever."

We'd entertained fruit flies for the past month, ever since I left a bowl of pears on the kitchen counter instead of putting them in the fridge. The pears were still good but the fruit flies were an annoying indication that we needed to eat them soon.

One did a kamikaze dive into my grandson's apple juice.

"Grandma, get him out. He's still swimming."

Not for long.

One spent the night in the toaster and flew out the next morning as the bread went in.

Fruit flies have staying power. They defy smushing and live out their short lives looking for something to eat and some place to multiply.

Apparently they ran out of food and, for now, we're down to one. We can live with that.

The problem really isn't the fruit flies. It's me. I need to use the fruit when I get it. Eat it, bake a pie, make a batch of jam or give it away—just don't let it sit unused.

"I think there's a spiritual application here."

Rich rolled his eyes. "Sometimes you push the envelope with your spiritual analogies."

"Well," I huffed. "You just never know when God wants to make a point."

I let the fruit fly matter drop.

Several weeks later the retreat committee at church asked me to teach a workshop. The topic? The Fruit of the Spirit. Bingo! I knew

God gave me those fruit flies for a reason. The Holy Spirit provides me with a wonderful basket of fruit—"love, joy, peace, patience, kindness, goodness, faithfulness, gentleness and self-control" (Galatians 5:22-23). Fruit meant to nourish, provide enjoyment, bless and encourage others—on and on.

What happens when I let this fruit sit unused and ignored? Spiritual fruit flies. Inconsiderate critters that buzz around my head, get stuck in my peanut butter toast and drown in my coffee as they pursue their own little fruit fly desires. My analogy breaks down here a bit as real fruit goes bad and fruit flies lay their eggs in it so the next generation gets a nutritious start. The Fruit of the Spirit, however, *never goes bad.* Spiritual fruit flies create stumbling blocks, distractions, temptations, bad habits, pitfalls—whatever it takes to keep me from nurturing and sharing the Spirit's fruit in my life. Paul describes some real doozies in Galatians 5:19-20:

> *The acts of the sinful nature are obvious: sexual immorality, impurity and debauchery; idolatry and witchcraft; hatred, discord, jealousy, fits of rage, selfish ambition, dissensions, factions and envy; drunkenness, orgies, and the like...*

Wow! Those are fruit flies on steroids.

I found it, a spiritual application! I could hardly wait to tell Rich.

It didn't take long, however, for God to burst the bubble of my enthusiasm. I soon realized I couldn't teach about the Fruit of the Spirit from a point of personal strength. I fell short in almost every area. I passed out a bit of fruit from time to time when I felt like it but it certainly wasn't a lifestyle. Most of my fruit had been in the bowl way too long. What was I going to do?

I searched the Scriptures and began to realize God's point. Christ chose me to bear fruit. Not of my own doing but through the indwelling of the Holy Spirit. The Spirit wants to use me to distribute His fruit *through* my life. I faced a crucial choice. I could continue to ignore the precious fruit God gave me until fruit flies began to appear (I already recognized a few—impatience, worry, procrastination, selfishness...) or I could tune-in to the Holy Spirit, look around me and pass it out. Such a simple truth, how did I miss it? Well, God's timing is perfect so if I'm a little slow on the uptake I figure He knows what He's doing.

Okay. I couldn't teach a workshop about something I believed to be a great plan of action if it wasn't *real* to me. God's call is to a daily, lifelong journey, going where He leads and loving what and who He loves. My feet were cold but my heart longed to follow the Spirit wherever He planned to lead me.

The workshop came together on schedule. We shared experiences and looked at the Fruit of the Spirit from a very practical perspective. God knows I love stories and lists. From all the stories, parables and lists in the Bible, I believe He does too. That's how the presentation came together, a relevant story, then a list of ideas on how to nurture and share each of the nine qualities of the Fruit of the Spirit. As usual, the teacher learned the most. Apparently, I needed to let God use me to write what I needed to learn. To show me how to let the Holy Spirit have His way in my life.

I expected to sit down and put my feet up after the class but my mind wouldn't shut off. More stories, more ideas. I wrote them down and tried them out. The only problem (a good one) was too much material for another workshop. I needed more room. With much encouragement from God, my husband and my writer's group, I decided to put it all together in a book. A practical book of ideas designed to encourage us to follow the Spirit's lead in the life He designed just for us as we give away the beautiful fruit He blesses us with while it's still fresh.

We'll always have fruit flies in our lives. They're persistent and adaptable. They know our soft spots. But don't give up. God's in the fruit business and He'll take care of them.

Please know this is not a book of legalistic do's and don'ts, although I occasionally use those words. This is a book of experiences from my life and stories from lives that bump into mine. God is using the events of my daily life to teach me to listen and respond to the Holy Spirit. To begin to nurture the Fruit of the Spirit in my life and then share it with others.

Thank you for coming with me as we make this journey together. I want you to *use* this book. Pick up a spiral notebook or journal and write out your thoughts, feelings, questions and nudges from the Spirit as you go along. Make it fun. If you're like me, I always think I'll go back and re-read and make notes but I never do. I need to keep a pen and notebook close at hand and use them. I get so much more out of a book if I take my time and write out notes. This practice collects my thoughts, creates new ones and helps me focus on what God wants to show me.

At the end of each chapter there is a Fruit for Thought section with questions for personal or group study. Each Fruit of the Spirit possesses a spiritual, internal dimension which produces a "walk the walk," external dimension. Therefore, you are also encouraged to begin to look closely at what the Holy Spirit is teaching you about His fruit in the stories of your own life.

We serve an amazing God who asks *His* children to bring *His* love and *His* light to *His* world. He created a mission for each of us. The fruit we share through our actions, attitudes and words contain the seeds of faith in Christ and eternal life to those who will receive it. God chose us to bear fruit, so let's open our hearts and our hands and God will continually fill them with a bounty of fruit to enjoy, as we give it away.

Before we begin this adventure, let's pray as the women prayed at that first workshop:

"Dear Lord, please open our eyes and ears to the voice and direction of Your Holy Spirit. Draw us into a close and teachable relationship. Create in us ready and yielded hearts. You have a different journey planned for each of us. The fruit is the same but the colors, shapes and flavors will be unique as You demonstrate Your glory in every life You touch. Thank You for this incredible and amazing challenge. Help us step out in faith knowing You will make it happen.

In Jesus Name, Amen."

FRUIT FOR THOUGHT

1. Make a list of all the Fruit Flies (stumbling blocks, pitfalls, distractions, temptations, etc.) you can think of in your culture and your personal life.

2. Look up "nurture" and "share" and related words, in a dictionary/thesaurus and write down as many synonyms as you can find. Put a star beside the actions you struggle with and a corresponding Fruit Fly. (i.e. *Nourish. Fruit Fly – busyness. Too busy to nourish the Fruit of the Spirit by spending consistent time in God's Word.)

3. Read Galatians 5:19-20 in at least two different versions of the Bible. Are there any descriptions that jump out at you? Any "ahas" or "yikes"?

Chapter One

THE FRUIT OF THE SPIRIT IS ... LOVE

A Journey with Dad

This is just a snapshot of how I learned the true meaning of love. The love we are meant to show one another—regardless of how we may feel. A tall order.

* * *

The room whirled and my stomach flipped. I'd managed a shower but staying upright to dry my hair was too much. Stress over taking Dad for a brain biopsy coupled with lack of sleep had awakened my dormant vertigo.

"Rich," I called. "I don't know if I can do this."

He bounded up the stairs from the kitchen, took one look at me with my wet head between my knees and said, "You're going back to bed."

"You can't go by yourself. Maybe if I take some more Dramamine I'll be OK."

"How many have you taken?"

"Three."

"You're not going anywhere. Your dad and I will be just fine."

"This isn't your job. I have to be there. What if Dad throws a fit?"

This was a token argument. I felt so sick and so relieved at the possibility of staying home I didn't really care about what I "should" be doing or how guilty I would feel later.

"If he loses it, I'll deal with it but I think he'll be fine. It's OK for you to let go of the controls once in a while. Charlie and I are big boys. We'll manage."

I let Rich lead me back to bed and tuck the covers around me.

"I know you were awake most of the night worrying so get some sleep. There's no point saying this but please don't feel guilty." He kissed me on the cheek and felt my damp hair.

"You're going to have a really bad hair day."

"Who cares," I mumbled as the room took another spin.

He kissed me again and turned to leave. I pulled the blanket from my face.

"Thank you so much, honey. You are so good to me, and to Dad. What would I do without you?"

"Well, hopefully, you won't have to find out. I love you. Now go to sleep."

I listened to the front door open and close then the familiar click of the lock. The car started, backed out of the driveway and Rich was gone.

It was 6:30 a.m. Dad had to be at the hospital early for a pre-surgery biopsy of his brain tumor. The doctors needed to know exactly what they were dealing with. This benign but invasive tumor had been a part of Dad's life for over forty years. Three previous surgeries had left him without his left eye and sinuses and no feeling on that side of his face. A three inch circle of skull had been removed and a question mark scar ran from his temple, around the top of his head and back to his ear. He wore a dark glass on the left side of his glasses to cover the bulge where his eye had been. He told curious children he was a pirate. Argggh!

The original surgeons didn't get all the tumor and it continued to grow, slowly but steadily, until my mother died. Then the tumor took off with a vengeance. Dad didn't want another surgery but as the tumor progressed and began to consume his face, he had no choice.

My father had always been hot-tempered and fifteen years caught in the web of alcoholism made matters worse. His only child, I knew he adored me. I loved him, but I lived in fear of his irrational and unpredictable anger. My fear didn't go away just because I grew up.

Dad's health declined so quickly after Mom's death he relied on Rich and me for almost all his needs. I quit my job to care for Dad, 8:00 to 10:00 in the morning and 3:00 to 5:00 in the afternoon with shopping and cooking in between. I didn't mind the errands and yard work and I certainly knew how to cook and clean. The trips with Dad to the doctor or the bank, or the barber, or anywhere public were another story. I never knew when he would explode at people or say awful things loud enough for all to hear. Or yell at me. I would be a wreck by the time I got home.

Rich came with me every afternoon on weekdays. Mornings, too, on the weekends. He and Dad never developed a close relationship but they always got along. Rich took care of my Dad as well as, or better than, any son would have.

He also kept me from tipping over the edge. My fear of my father and emotional exhaustion were taking their toll. My marbles were falling out at an alarming rate and Rich's unfailing love, his humor, his male perspective and his endless patience kept me functioning.

Now, I don't want you to think Rich is a saint. That would be annoying and hard to live with. He frequently commented as we pulled away from Dad's house in the afternoon, "He's quite a handful, you know that don't you?"

"Yes, I know. But he's ours."

He could always share a "Dad story" in a way that would make me laugh. Not out of disrespect for Dad but simply to help us keep things in perspective. We needed to lighten up once in a while. On occasion he could even make Dad laugh.

※ ※ ※

I woke up when the phone rang at 1:00 p.m.

"Hello," I mumbled.

"Hey, it's Dad. How are you feeling?"

"Hi Daddy. I think I'm better. How are you? I'm so sorry I couldn't go with you today."

"I'm fine, just tired and worried about you."

Was I dreaming? This didn't sound like my father.

"Rich and I had to wait for two *%#&* hours until I finally got in. The biopsy didn't take long but they made me stay in recovery for a while. I don't think any of those *%#&* doctors know what they're doing."

No, I was awake. This was Dad.

"That husband of yours took good care of me. He fixed a big plate of scrambled eggs and toast and made a fresh pot of coffee when we got home. He's up at Safeway now picking up my prescriptions. I just wanted to check on you and let you know we were back."

"I should feel good enough to come over later with your dinner."

I sat up and swung my legs over the side of the bed. No dizziness. I felt pretty good.

"No, you stay home. Rich is picking up a sandwich at the deli for my dinner. I'll see you tomorrow."

"OK, Dad, if you're sure. Call me during the night if you need anything. I love you."

"You just get well. See you in the morning." Click.

I guess I'm not as indispensable as I thought.

I passed the full-length mirror as I headed for the bathroom. Yikes! Rich was right—I looked like a demented squirrel. I really should save the hair for him, he'd enjoy it, but my female pride wouldn't let me. I showered again, did my hair, got dressed and waited for Rich to come home. I was sure he had some stories Dad hadn't shared.

I saw love lived out right in front of me during the two years Rich and I took care of Dad.

- ♦ Through Dad's fits of temper in doctor's offices to middle of the night trips to the emergency room, Rich remained steady and calm (even the night he broke his toe trying to get his pants on in the dark).

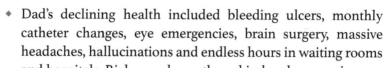

- Dad's declining health included bleeding ulcers, monthly catheter changes, eye emergencies, brain surgery, massive headaches, hallucinations and endless hours in waiting rooms and hospitals. Rich was always there, kind and supportive.
- Rich maintained Dad's house, and ours, and sat for hours shrouded in second-hand cigarette smoke watching CNN and visiting with Dad. (Rich doesn't smoke and can only take so much news). His patience and endurance buoyed Dad and me up and kept us going.
- The day my father went to the hospital for the final time, he wanted a bath. He needed to sit in a chair as he could no longer climb in and out of the tub. Rich went in to help. The door was cracked open and I saw my father bracing himself on Rich's shoulders as Rich knelt before him washing my father's feet.

My husband lived out selfless love toward a difficult, angry and frightened man. Did Rich feel like caring for my Dad? Probably not. Would he rather have been doing something else? Playing golf? Undoubtedly. Yet he showed up every day for two years and stood faithfully at his father-in-law's bedside the night Dad passed away. His love never failed.

My father's been gone for twelve years. I will never forget the strong foundation Rich created for two frightened people. I could have read endlessly about how God expects us to love and never really gotten it. It took an ordinary man (he's not ordinary to me) to demonstrate the extraordinary truth of the power of love lived out through a human life.

Love is patient, love is kind. It does not envy, it does not boast, it is not proud.
It is not rude, it is not self-seeking, it is not easily angered,
it keeps no record of wrongs.
Love does not delight in evil but rejoices with the truth.
It always protects, always trusts, always hopes, always perseveres.
Love never fails.
1 Corinthians 13:4-8

Love

Nurturing Fruit

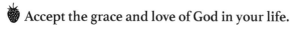 **Accept the grace and love of God in your life.**

Why is it often so hard to believe in God's unmerited love and forgiveness? Oh, we say we do while at the same time we lug around a
generous portion of guilt and shame. We often feel unworthy of love,
especially God's, but God makes it pretty clear that He wants us to
accept His love and forgiveness just like a little child.

> *...I tell you the truth, unless you change and become like little
> children, you will never enter the kingdom of heaven.*
> Matthew 18:3

Read the verse one more time and let it sink in. Do you feel a
weight being lifted off you? I hope so. That's all the "stuff" that doesn't
belong in a child's life. The stuff that keeps the fruit flies buzzing
around our heads. The extra weight that makes it hard for the Holy
Spirit to get anything done through us.

When my oldest grandson was little I don't remember him wandering around feeling unloved and guilty about his bad choices. He
would say he was sorry (sometimes under duress) and receive the
consequences. A love and snuggle were sometimes required. My
mischief maker may not have been happy about being found out but
he didn't question the love of the one who caught him in the act (that
will come when he's a teenager). This happened repeatedly throughout the day and yet the child went to bed feeling loved and secure
with a clear conscience. Sometimes, if he didn't get "caught," he confessed on his own. I'm probably reading too much into a small child's

psyche but guilt (unconfessed sin) doesn't feel good and he wanted it to go away. Solution: tell on yourself (confess), say you're sorry (ask forgiveness), deal with it (repent), feel better and go out to play (or go to bed and sleep tight).

I realize life becomes more complicated as we grow. The business of living in this world and the pain, temptations, failures and successes we experience often draw us away from the profound simplicity of God's message:

For God so loved the world that he gave his one and only Son, that whoever believes in him shall not perish but have eternal life.
John 3:16

It takes the faith of a little child to accept a "no matter what" kind of love, trust the totality of forgiveness, learn our lessons, sniff up our tears and go happily on our way. So lighten up. You and I are children (a.k.a. sinners) and we always will be, but we have a great God who is bigger than our sin, knows everything about us and loves us anyway. A God who keeps us growing closer to the image of His Son. Love, forgiveness, freedom and the amazing grace of God are ours for the asking.

🍓 Forgive so you can love.

The internal work of forgiveness can be hard but it's one of the greatest ways we can express love. Remember, it's a choice not a feeling and is based on the forgiveness and love God has shown us. That should be enough but it's still hard. Here are a few things God has pointed out to me:

   ◆ Let things go—don't hold grudges. I have come to realize that I rather like gnawing on a good grudge. Like a dog with a bone. What a waste of time and energy (for me not the dog). Some hurts are intentional and may require some action, but after giving it some thought, I'd hazard a guess that most of the things that upset me are unintentional or simply not worth headspace. Let it go! I'm embarrassed to admit it but there are times I go looking for a hurt so I can be the "victim." Woe is me. This is a crummy thing to do to the poor soul you choose to have inflicted the imagined infraction. They have no idea what they did. This leads to distrust and emotional distance, and who can blame them. I've "walked on eggshells" around a few of these victim-types and I don't want to cause anyone to tiptoe around me.

♦ Avoid pity parties. They can be fun (that's why they're called parties) and become a hard habit to break. Be aware of where your mind is going in its down time and re-direct it if it's stewing about something it shouldn't. Making the bed and cleaning house (when my mind is disengaged) are favorite times for me to *enjoy* mental arguments or hash over old hurts. Sometimes the person I'm arguing with is dead! I try to remember to sing or listen to music (ear buds are helpful) to keep my mind occupied. Remember, love doesn't hang out at pity parties.

♦ Give your unforgiveness to God and ask Him to heal it. One of my first life changes as a new believer involved forgiveness. I experienced repeated nightmares in which I strangled a person I loved dearly but was very angry with (my husband asked me to mention it wasn't him). These dreams were extremely upsetting and I asked God to take them away. He reminded me of all I had been forgiven and asked me to forgive. I made a conscious choice to forgive and the dream stopped. God answered my prayer and the dream never returned. He not only took away the anger, He gradually replaced it with a deeper, compassionate love.

Forgiveness is a lifelong process. There will always be something. A real or perceived wrong, unkind words, the injustice of the world we live in, our own weakness or inadequacy, on and on. We need to rely on God to remind us when forgiveness is needed and to give us the strength to follow through by the power of His love.

I read a sign in a shop the other day that made me think. "If you want to know where your heart is—look where your mind goes when it wanders." If my mind is wading through muddy grudges, headed to pity-parties or avoiding God, I have unforgiveness in my heart.

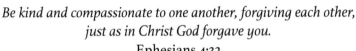

Be kind and compassionate to one another, forgiving each other,
just as in Christ God forgave you.
Ephesians 4:32

🍓 Read and memorize God's Word.

I know you've been told to read your Bible a jillion times but, for my own benefit, I'm going to make it a jillion and one. The Bible is God's Holy Word and the primary way He speaks to us. When I was a new believer I was excited to read my Bible. God used it to speak His thoughts and convey His love to *me*. Each verse I memorized (not an easy undertaking for me!) has blessed me over and over again, popping into my brain exactly when needed.

I experienced a season when I began to lose my excitement for God's Word. I still read Scripture most days but I missed my old anticipation as I picked up my Bible. I rarely attempted to memorize a verse. Why did this happen? I don't have a good answer. Laziness, familiarity, busyness, disobedience, maybe a touch of depression, and who knows what other "fruit flies" contributed to my spiritual "hardening of the arteries." But as surely as unseen clogged arteries can stop a beating heart, the gradual slowing of spiritual disciplines can stop the Holy Spirit's movement in and through a life. Mine. God really got my attention on this one!

The excuse "I'm just not disciplined," doesn't fly. I get up on time (most days), shower and brush my teeth. The morning routine. I've disciplined myself because it's good for me and makes me feel good. You do the same thing. We each have many examples of discipline in our lives. Studying and learning God's Word is good for us and leads to spiritual health. Ever forget to brush your teeth? You feel yucky all day. If you regularly spend time listening and learning with God through His Word, you'll notice if you miss a day. His Word is a "lamp to my feet and a light for my path" (Psalm 119:105) and "thoroughly equips me for every good work" (2 Tim. 3:17 NASB). I don't know about you but I need all the light and equipping I can get. I started to pray for a renewed joy in God's Word and, as I waited, I read. I began to realize my diet of God's Word is what causes His life to flow through me. My feelings still ride the ups and downs of life's roller coaster but an over-riding sense of God's love and the power of His Word in my life returned.

Memorizing Scripture is hard and takes practice. I don't particularly like to practice. I had a terrible time with the multiplication tables and still stumble on the eights and nines. From piano lessons to Spanish classes, I didn't practice so I didn't learn. I didn't possess the "want to." However, I've known the Lord's Prayer and the Twenty-third Psalm as long as I can remember. Did Grandma teach me? I have no idea when I memorized them but their presence in my brain tells me I'm quite capable of learning. Those Scriptures are ingrained in me and I take them with me wherever I go. Whatever I may face I can find strength, love and encouragement from my Father's words "hidden...in my heart" (Psalm 119:11). I have the "want to" for learning Scripture. I simply need to begin. It's hard to remember Scripture if you're not applying it to your life. Choose a verse, or a passage of Scripture, to memorize that relates to your current situation, and live with it for a while. Keep practicing and it will soon take root and be firmly planted in your mind.

I just need to be careful I don't enthusiastically set up a "system" and then never do anything with it. I once created an elaborate file card system for Scripture memorization with a section for each book of the Bible. I got the idea from a friend who had a shoebox crammed with file cards of verses she had *actually memorized*. I think my box was cuter than hers but after about a year it only held six cards and I couldn't say those verses without cheating.

❋ ❋ ❋

You may not have experienced spiritual doldrums or difficulty memorizing Scripture as I have. I hope not. But if you have and you want a return to spiritual health, ask God to help you long for Him, make you conscious of your need for His love, and pick up His Book.

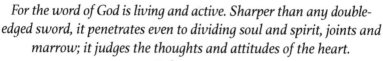

For the word of God is living and active. Sharper than any double-edged sword, it penetrates even to dividing soul and spirit, joints and marrow; it judges the thoughts and attitudes of the heart.
Hebrews 4:12

Let the word of Christ dwell in you richly...
Colossians 3:16a

 Pray

I own twelve books specifically on prayer. I went through all our bookshelves and counted. I've read them all. This doesn't include books with chapters devoted to prayer which I have also read. I have prayer journals, prayer lists, specific systems and techniques for prayer and have attended Bible studies devoted to prayer. These are all good things yet I regularly suffer from prayerlessness.

I know what part of my problem is. I love to set goals and make lists and create timelines, but I'm a bit unreliable with the follow-through. I enjoy buying all the supplies for a new undertaking but when it starts to get too hard or too time consuming or too expensive I give up and move on. Let's see—sewing, watercolor painting, guitar, furniture refinishing, horseback riding, quilting, exercising—you get the picture.

We all have different temperaments, personalities, gifts and styles. Individual strengths and weaknesses. God made unique individuals so He would have someone available for whatever He needs done. Plus, we're much more interesting that way. However, regardless of our particular bent, God gives us each the ability to hear His voice and speak directly to Him. We are, after all, His little children. Ask Him to reveal your individuality and to re-light the inner fire to keep you coming daily to the throne of grace. Ask Him to help you long for intimacy with Him. He will teach you to trust and fill you with His love. Prayer is a privilege and the most powerful weapon we possess. Use it.

I'm not going to tell you how to pray. You probably have a shelf full of books of your own. I would like to quote Brother Lawrence from *Practicing the Presence of God.* "It is a great delusion to think our times of prayer ought to differ from other times. We are as strictly obliged to cleave to God by action in the time of action as by prayer in the season of prayer." In other words, pray without ceasing. Whether in our daily retreat with God or in the busyness of our day, God wants to be part of everything we do, wherever we are. If we are willing to dedicate every area of our lives to prayer, who knows what God will do! He loves to hear us pray. No elaborate words or required word count. Just talk, He's listening.

Be joyful always; pray continually; give thanks in all circumstances,
for this is God's will for you in Christ Jesus.
1 Thessalonians 5:16-18

Confess and repent to keep your love light shining.

Keep short accounts with God. When we goof up, the Holy Spirit gives our conscience a poke and we feel it. Ouch! We have the choice to ignore the Spirit or immediately confess it to God and ask Him to help us keep from repeating the sin. We don't have to go looking for transgressions under every rock, we all have enough obvious sins to keep us busy. Stay alert for the Holy Spirit's elbow in your side and respond quickly.

Several years ago the entire family gathered at our house for Thanksgiving. I had been cleaning for a week but there were still several fruit flies buzzing around the kitchen. My youngest son had flown home from Hawaii and stood in the kitchen with most of the other guests as I tried to clear a path so I could finish dinner. Suddenly, in a loud voice he announced, "Hey Mom, I know why you have fruit flies. Look at all the slime in your garbage disposal. When was the last time you cleaned this thing?" I turned, along with everyone else, to see him holding the black stopper and peering into the drain. This child possessed impeccable timing. He worked in a restaurant and, apparently, this was a problem he was familiar with. I gave him the fisheye and said with as much composure as I could muster, "Well, maybe after dinner you could clean it for me, *Sweetie.*"

As I remember this story one of the "woe to you" verses Jesus spoke to the Pharisees came to mind.

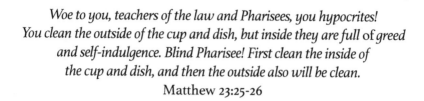

Woe to you, teachers of the law and Pharisees, you hypocrites!
You clean the outside of the cup and dish, but inside they are full of greed
and self-indulgence. Blind Pharisee! First clean the inside of
the cup and dish, and then the outside also will be clean.
Matthew 23:25-26

Keep the disposal clean (confession) and the fruit flies out of the kitchen.

If we confess our sins, He is faithful and righteous to forgive us our sins
and to cleanse us from all unrighteousness.
1 John 1:9 NASB

What about those entrenched sins we want to give to God but can't quite let go of? They're like old friends at the tavern (just a metaphor). We know they're not good for us but we've known them for a long time and enjoy their company. "C'mon God, let me keep this one." Fortunately, God loves us too much to let us have everything we want.

Parting with "oldie but goodie" sins is hard and often hurts. I have asked God over and over to change my stubborn, childish heart and help me let go of those sins I hang on to as if they were my best friends. He tells me to get off the bar stool (whatever it may represent in my life) and walk out of the tavern. I want Him to fix me, Zap! He wants me to trust Him enough to surrender and turn away. He will strengthen my steps as I go. He and I have walked this path to freedom more than once. I'm finally realizing that matching my will against God's is a dumb move and am finding it easier to let go and reach for His hand. He hasn't dropped me yet and has blessed me with freedom, compassion for others and a love I never thought would be mine.

Leaving the darkness we hold so tightly may require counseling or a support group but it is a spiritual battle and definitely requires God's intervention. It can be a long process but if we confess and turn away from the sin (over and over if necessary) and surrender our helpless selves, God will heal us from the inside out. His love brightens the light and the love in our hearts.

Who can discern his errors? Forgive my hidden faults. Keep your servant also from willful sins; may they not rule over me. Then will I be blameless, innocent of great transgression.
Psalm 19:12-13

Love

Sharing Fruit

 Pass God's love and grace onto others.

Earlier we looked at accepting God's grace in *our* lives. Now we need to turn around and demonstrate His grace to others. Showing grace isn't always easy so we need to pay attention to what is going on around us and how we are going to react.

If we look for ways to extend God's loving grace we will see them everywhere. The inexperienced grocery checker or the woman with forty coupons you didn't notice before you unloaded your cart. The forgotten birthday, thoughtless words, the overdue repairman, the gum-snapping receptionist, the lady who steals your parking space. The list of opportunities for grace is endless. God must feel the same way about us.

When we show God's grace and love to others, they often show grace to the next person and eventually it comes back to us. Even if it doesn't, God says do it.

This is my command: Love each other.
John 15:17

It has been my experience that showing grace opens me up to God's love. It frees me from anger and bitterness and brings light into my life. I want that light. Refusing to show God's grace, whether in big issues or my daily run-in with humanity, allows a darkness to grow in me. Big fruit flies can hatch there. I don't want this darkness in me, waiting to be fed. Creepy!

It's so much better to ask the Holy Spirit to shine His light in the gloomy recesses of my soul and show me when and how to drop loving, daily graces into the lives that touch mine. If I follow the Spirit's lead, life is a lot more fun and much less stressful.

...I am the light of the world. Whoever follows will never walk
in the darkness, but will have the light of life.
John 8:12

🍓 **Let yourself be genuine, transparent and a bit vulnerable with people.**

Love requires letting people see the real you. The good and the not so good. You don't need to spill your guts with everyone you meet but being honest and transparent frees others to be real with you. It's such a relief to meet someone who admits they don't have it all together. None of us do but most of us are "pretty good" at looking "pretty good." How exhausting!

Now, I'll admit that if every time someone asked, "How are you doing?" we told them—at length—they would eventually quit asking. We don't need to overdo it but hiding behind masks and pretending everything is great when it isn't isolates us from each other and the give and take of God's love and grace.

I've been privileged to attend the co-dependency class at Celebrate Recovery, a Christian twelve-step program. I needed to leave my masks at the door and enter in. The people I met were honest and open. The worship simple and sweet. The leadership accessible and caring. Tangible grace. I felt safe and able to accept grace and love from others and give grace and love in return.

Let's go on a "grace mission" in our corner of the world. Be willing to let the Holy Spirit take you outside your comfort zone. God doesn't like you camped there anyway. Be touchable. Be willing to be interrupted. Be available. Imitate Jesus' loving interaction with people, all the people, He puts in your path.

I have an old stuffed tiger named Pepito. My Aunt Norma bought him for my third birthday. (Yikes, he's getting old!) She let me choose and I spent a *long* time looking at all the animals. I refused all her suggestions until I saw the tiger with the sad eyes. Aunt Norma liked the black panther better but couldn't talk me out of the tiger. He belonged with me. Pepito currently resides on our dresser (Rich gives him a poke now and then just to get me riled up. I think he's jealous). Pepito's fur is all rubbed off (like *The Velveteen Rabbit*). His felt nose disappeared long ago, his head flops and his eyes hang loose. Letting me love him was risky business. I still reach for him when I'm sad or scared. I *really do know* he's a stuffed animal and, maybe it's silly, but he's a touchable example of God's grace to the little girl in me. Pepito is only real in my mind. His love and acceptance and unconditional grace imagined. But I believe God gave me that dear old tiger to give the security and grace I desperately needed until I realized it was God's grace all along. I pray God gives me the courage and heart to be a Pepito to the people in my life who need one.

...live a life of love, just as Christ loved us and gave himself up for us as a fragrant offering and sacrifice to God.
Ephesians 5:2

🍓 **Show love as you anticipate people's needs.**

Rich and I sat in the waiting room after my mother's stroke. TV news and old magazines to pass the time until we could talk to the doctor.

Suddenly, three women with tender smiles filled the room with hugs, tears and simple words of comfort. An envoy of friends from my Bible study. They brought a basket filled with water bottles, snacks, new magazines, a crossword puzzle book, journal and pen, note cards and stamps, and a card filled with words of love and encouragement from all the girls.

They visited for a few minutes, prayed for Mom, passed out another round of hugs and said, "Good-bye." They left but the light they brought with them stayed.

The basket of goodies was great and certainly met physical and entertainment needs but the gift we appreciated most was the act of love. These friends thought about our situation and went into action. They didn't say, "Call us if you need anything." They put themselves in our place and met what they believed to be our immediate need. Rich and I felt less isolated and frightened as our friends came alongside and made the burden we carried a bit lighter.

As I remember this story, I recall the saying, "People may not remember what you said but they will never forget that you came." I haven't forgotten.

❋ ❋ ❋

When we saw the doctor he told us Mom suffered two massive strokes. She wasn't expected to live. I spent the night in the ICU waiting area. There were several people keeping vigil over loved ones in the darkened room. During the night a young woman came and covered me with a blanket. I thought she was a volunteer.

The next morning I asked a nurse about her.

"Jane's husband has been in ICU for over a week," the nurse said as her voice softened. "They're from out of town and their four children are staying with her brother's family. She spends the day at Tom's side and does what she can for the others in the waiting room at night."

Unable to travel home, the nurses allowed Jane to sleep in an alcove off the waiting room. I walked by hoping to meet her but found the tiny room empty except for a few clothes in a duffel bag and an open Bible on her cot.

In the middle of her own fear and loneliness Jane silently served her Lord and proclaimed Jesus by anticipating and meeting the needs of the lives she touched within the circle of her circumstances. I know you get my point but I want to share a few more thoughts:

– 17 –

- When it occurs to you to do something helpful, do it. If I got credit for good intentions I'd be a saint, but I'm not. Too often I let the moment for action pass and whatever God wanted to do through *me* didn't happen.
- Be the difference. You may be the only one who reaches out actively to a person or family in need. Don't assume someone else will do it. God chose you.
- Plan ahead. Make a list of what would be needed in different situations so you don't have to "think" in the middle of a crisis.
- Stock up on note cards. Encouraging handwritten words can bring comfort and connection. E-mails and texts are great too, but there is something special about taking the time to share your thoughts and feelings in your own hand. Plus, everyone loves to get mail or a note tucked in a gift.
- Enlist help if a need is too big for you. If God wants something done, He has the people and resources available.

God doesn't ask us to take care of the whole world, but He does expect us to move into action when He brings a specific need to our attention. Let's keep our eyes and ears open in anticipation of God's next assignment.

And the King will answer and say to them, "Truly I say to you, to the extent that you did it to one of these brothers of Mine, even the least of them, you did it to Me."
Matthew 25:40

🍓 **Demonstrate love by taking the initiative in relationships.**
Webster's New World Dictionary defines initiative as "the action of taking the first step or move…" In a relationship it means make the phone call, extend the invitation, start the conversation.

Sad to say, this is not my strong suit. I enjoy people and love to spend time with friends and family. I'm also an introvert and quite happy on my own puttering around, entertaining myself. Maybe this comes from being an only child, who knows? My mother was the same way. Left to her own devices, she tended to be a loner with her nose in a library book. However, her friends enjoyed her company and kept her social calendar full with no effort on her part.

Shortly after Mom died, one of her close friends said to me, "You know, Annie, I loved Betty and I know she loved me. She was my best friend, but in all the years I knew her, she never called me. I always called her." I didn't know what to say but an alarm went off inside my head.

I rarely call friends just to chat, forget to check e-mails and am slow to respond (forget Facebook!) I hardly ever organize a get-together or extend an invitation to lunch. Why?

* Busyness. Life is busy and often way too crowded. If we don't have time to maintain relationships, jettison some activities and habits (TV, recreational shopping, internet, whatever). Having been a female for sixty-plus years I'm very sympathetic to women's crazy schedules and the demands put on us by work, family, our house, ourselves, and a jillion other valid (or not so valid) obligations and activities. But, something's got to give so we have time to nurture and be nurtured by those we love.

* Fear of rejection. What if I reach out and the other person turns down my invitation or doesn't have time to talk. So what? This isn't rejection, its life. Rejection is, "Go away, I do not like you." Keep trying.

* Laziness. Social interaction takes a bit of effort and is easy to put off. So...make the call when you think of it. Answer the e-mail promptly. Occasionally be the one to organize an activity. Start a conversation with a new person at church. Don't dilly-dally around or it will never happen. I have friends and relatives who don't have a problem in this area and keep me in the loop but that doesn't get me off the hook. Relationships need to be tended or they begin to wither. Some people will hang-in there and keep you close but others give up and drift away. How sad and how easily avoided.

Anyone, then, who knows the good he ought to do and doesn't do it, sins.
James 4:17

Note: In the middle of editing this chapter, a dear friend and sister in Christ died suddenly. She experienced a difficult life and occasionally expressed her desire to spend a day at the beach together walking and talking. Due to circumstances, I needed to make this happen and, caught up in a busy schedule, I didn't. God forgive me for this simple act of love I didn't give.

🍓 **Pray actively for others.**

When you say, "I'll pray for you," do it. Right then, if possible. I learned this by example. "In the moment" prayers didn't come naturally to me, or even occur to me until I saw them in action.

- A fairly new Christian, I was having coffee with a friend from church. I mentioned an area I struggled with in my faith. She reached across the table, took my hand and said, "Let's pray about it," and she did, right there in the coffee shop! She wasn't long-winded and didn't make a big deal out of it, just lifted my concern to God, gave my hand a squeeze and reached for her coffee.

- My friend, Bonnie, taught me to pray in the car. Whenever she saw an ambulance or fire truck with their siren on, she would pull over and pray for everyone involved. If her boys were with her, they prayed too. I was impressed and encouraged to pursue this type of prayer outreach. Emergency vehicles, accidents, panhandlers, people waiting for the bus in the rain, the guy next to us at the red light—the opportunities for prayer as we travel through our days are many.

- What about when we aren't driving around? I can send up a prayer for the young mother in the store with two fussy kiddos, or the woman sighing unhappily in the next dressing room at the department store (probably trying on bathing suits). How about the couple arguing (or ignoring each other) in the restaurant? They could probably use a prayer.

We simply need to keep our eyes and hearts open so we're ready to respond with prayer when the Holy Spirit gives us a nudge. We don't have to know what the need is. God does. He simply tells us to pray.

Immediate prayers don't wait to get on the Prayer Chain or your personal prayer list (although both of these are very good destinations). They are spontaneous and happen at the moment of felt need. I don't understand how God uses our prayers or why they possess such power but I want to be part of whatever He is up to and prayer (in any form, at any time) is His invitation to join Him.

Pray, then, in this way: Our Father who art in heaven, Hallowed be Thy name. Thy kingdom come. Thy will be done, on earth as it is in heaven. Give us this day our daily bread. And forgive us our debts, as we also have forgiven our debtors. And do not lead us into temptation, but deliver us from evil.
Matthew 6:9-13 NASB

FRUIT FOR THOUGHT

Love

Nurturing Fruit

1. Describe a time you were touched by God's love demonstrated through another person.

2. Do you ever struggle accepting God's grace in your life? Can you see the little girl He sees and trust His simple message of forgiveness and eternal life? Is there anything you need to let go of?

3. Do you have a problem with grudges, pity parties or forgiveness? Write about a time you decided to let an offence

go and forgive. How did it feel? Write about a time you were forgiven. How did that feel?

4. What do you think about the sections on reading and memorizing God's word? Are there any changes you need or want to make in your spiritual disciplines?

5. How would you define "pray without ceasing?" How can you incorporate this into your life?

6. Do you keep short accounts with God? Are there any areas in your life you have trouble truly repenting and giving up? This can be a long, difficult process but what does God have waiting for you when you finally let go?

Sharing Fruit

1. Can you identify any "fruit flies" in your life that have hatched from lack of love and grace? Make a list of ways you can drop "daily graces" into the lives you touch. What would a "grace mission" look like in your corner of the world? Be creative.

2. Are you "pretty good" at looking "pretty good?" How do you feel when you think of being "genuine, transparent and a bit vulnerable?" How would this change your relationships?

3. What are two things you could do this week to reach out to others by anticipating their needs? Make a list of practical things you could do for people in different situations. Is there a need God has placed before you that you're trying to ignore? If God wills it He will give you the ability to do it. Anything come to mind?

4. Is there an area or a person in your life where you are neglecting love? How would you feel at the end of your life if this continues? How can you begin to reverse the neglect and renew the love?

5. List three ways you can develop the practice of immediate prayers for others. Then do them.

❋ ❋ ❋

Grab your notebook and write out...

◆ One Scripture from this chapter that is particularly meaningful to you.

◆ Your Thoughts and Stories

❋ ❋ ❋

Chapter Two

THE FRUIT OF THE SPIRIT IS … JOY

The Run-in

I was in a snit. The telepathic "let's go out for dinner" messages aimed at my husband, Rich, were not being received. It was getting late. I needed to take action.

"What would you like for dinner, honey?" I asked, trying to sound tired.

"Spaghetti sounds good," he answered without stopping to think. This was his usual fallback position for dinner ideas.

I sighed—twice. I didn't want him to miss it.

"Are you okay?"

"Sure," I said, slipping into my martyr role. "I have to run to the store. Be back in a bit." I scowled, grabbed the car keys and closed the back door very firmly on my way out.

I walked into the store, yanked a grocery cart out of the line-up and grumbled to myself as I plowed up and down the aisles. A jar of spaghetti sauce, a can of mushrooms, bread, pasta—nothing home-made tonight—and no meat! I was in full passive/aggressive mode.

Paying no attention to my fellow shoppers, I charged out of the canned food aisle and broadsided another cart. The driver, a little old man who hung on gamely as his cart lurched sideways, wore khaki slacks and a blue plaid shirt. He looked to be in his eighties.

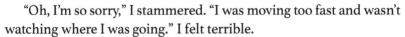

"Oh, I'm so sorry," I stammered. "I was moving too fast and wasn't watching where I was going." I felt terrible.

The old gentleman grinned at me. "That's OK dear. No harm done. I don't mind being hit by such a pretty young woman. You have yourself a nice day."

"Thank you for being so kind. You have a good day, too." I smiled weakly.

"Oh I will. I usually do." He headed off past the milk coolers.

I turned the other way then stopped and looked behind me to make sure my victim was really okay. His back was to me but I noticed everyone he passed slowed down and smiled. The butcher stocking the meat case stopped to chat.

My mood began to lift and the verse from Proverbs 17:22 came to mind. "A cheerful heart is good medicine..." Well, this fellow was certainly cheerful and seemed to make everyone he met feel better.

The next verse God dropped into my brain was Philippians 2:14, "Do all things without grumbling or disputing" (NASB). Hmmm...I wasn't looking good in this comparison.

I took a deep breath and decided to lighten up. Why was I upset? By expecting my husband to know what I wanted instead of just telling him, I was setting myself up for disappointment and, I hate to admit it, the enjoyment of playing the martyr.

OK, Lord. I'm starting to get the message.

Proceeding to the pet food aisle I smiled at a woman with her head tipped back reading the labels through her bifocals.

"Too many choices," she muttered.

"I know. I don't know why I bother," I said. "Betsy turns up her nose whatever I feed her."

"Same with my Sam." She shook her head. We chatted about our finicky cats then, laughing, continued our shopping.

At the checkout I caught sight of the gentleman again. I wasn't in the same line but I could see that he and the clerk were laughing. He even had the sullen box boy smiling.

As I watched him walk out the door, I wondered how many people running a routine errand today found themselves grinning? First at him and then at the next person they met? How many gloomy moods had been lifted? How many people had been touched and changed by his cheerful attitude and generous smiles? I know one person was.

I pulled into the garage with a much better attitude than when I'd pulled out. I smiled a "real" smile at Rich as I walked past him toting grocery bags.

"Anything else in the car?" he asked, getting off the couch.

"Just one more bag."

He headed for the garage and returned munching on a hunk of French bread, dribbling crumbs.

My smile widened. It was our practice that a baguette never made it home from the store intact. I had apparently been too preoccupied with my run-in to remember to put the bread up front with me. Rich set the bag down and began unloading.

"Hey," he mumbled through bread crumbs. "You seemed a little tense when you left. Why don't we save the spaghetti for tomorrow and go out tonight? Sound good?"

"Sounds very good," I answered, laughing. "You read my mind."

Thank you, Lord, for my dear husband and for knowing how much I needed that trip to the store today.

Joy

Nurturing Fruit

Choose joy.

First of all, I want to be careful not to confuse joy and happiness. While they differ in expression, I have come to believe they are flip sides of the same coin.

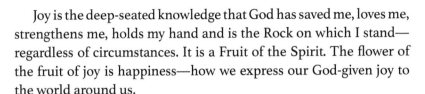
Joy is the deep-seated knowledge that God has saved me, loves me, strengthens me, holds my hand and is the Rock on which I stand—regardless of circumstances. It is a Fruit of the Spirit. The flower of the fruit of joy is happiness—how we express our God-given joy to the world around us.

I used to think happiness existed apart from joy and depended entirely on circumstances. I felt happy with my grandson asleep in my arms, or new furniture, or a batch of kittens tumbling through the house. My happiness depended on life going my way. Sounded good.

But what happens when the grandson wakes up and yells, "I want my "Mommy," and the kittens shred the side of the new sofa? Poof! My happiness disappears. Should it? I don't think so. I may react to circumstances and my feelings may differ with the ups and downs of life, but my underlying attitude should flow from the joy within me. If I depend solely on the emotion of happiness I miss out on the deep, abiding joy God has prepared for me. I can certainly choose to depend on the world, other people, the weather, a good hair day, whatever, for my happiness, but those things are often fleeting and unreliable. Real happiness doesn't just happen, it blossoms and flowers when we choose to sink our roots into the rich soil of joy the Holy Spirit nourishes in our hearts.

I have friends who breathe in God's joy like fresh air. They are delightful, cheerful-hearted souls. They are not thin skinned and rarely take themselves too seriously. I know these women have their share of problems (and sometimes more) but they walk close to God and it shows in their attitude. They possess joy and have chosen cheerful hearts. Their humor is appropriate and their tears real.

These same women are warm, caring and capable of deep compassion. They have balance. Being cheerful all the time, regardless of what others are feeling is selfish, defies God's plan and can be very insensitive. We need to be realistically upbeat in matters that pertain to us and very sensitive to how God wants us to react to others.

I have thought a lot about these women because I am not one of them. I am not naturally perky. I easily let my thoughts and actions be ruled by my feelings. I often make myself and everyone around me miserable when I have so much to be thankful for and so much beauty in my life to share. I know I possess the joy of the Lord but too often don't choose to live like it.

This is one of those "chicken and the egg" things. Which comes first, the inward attitude or the outward cheerfulness? When money is tight, my jeans tighter, and my marbles loose, I don't feel particularly chipper. But when I rely on the joy of the Lord and choose to act pleasant anyway (and sometimes it's a real effort) I usually begin to feel better. Pretty soon my cheerful heart is the real deal. Heart healing and attitude adjustments begin with God and when we cooperate, He uses us to spread His healing joy to others.

I realize life can throw some awful things our way and sometimes joy is nowhere in sight, let alone happiness. Joy can run deep, sort of like a submarine, beneath the waves of our circumstances, but given enough time it will surface. You may not be able to feel it for a season, maybe a long season, but God has not forgotten you and His joy is alive.

As I sit here staring at my computer, I realize I need the joy of the Lord to be my default position. Regardless of soaring highs or plunging depths of emotion (and its okay to feel what I feel as long as I don't camp there) I need to return to the constant, sustaining joy of the Lord that runs through the center of my soul. God's joy will keep me from depending on worldly pleasures or succumbing to sorrow. I need to make up my mind.

God lets us choose—so choose His joy.

Rejoice in the Lord always. I will say it again: Rejoice!
Philippians 4:4

If you're a grumbler, whiner, or complainer—STOP!

We all get to bellyache and vent once in a while. We are human after all. Sometimes a genuine issue or concern is alleviated by sharing and seeking advice. However, if we chronically grumble, whine and complain, we need to knock it off.

Paul tells us in James 5:9, "Don't grumble against each other... " Nothing can pop your balloon, rain on your parade and suck the joy right out of a room (or a life) like a negative, habitual complainer. At best these people annoy and exhaust others and tend to be avoided. At worst they break up friendships, marriages and churches. Grumblers create their own gloomy cycle. "Everything is wrong, nobody likes me, woe is me. I'll fix them." Around it goes.

I'm not talking about people whose problems stem from their childhood or those who suffer from depression or other illnesses. I'm addressing those of us who have developed a bad habit. Complaining and grumbling are rooted in pride and feed a subtle need to feel like a victim and manipulate others. It doesn't work. At least not for long.

Many years ago I worked with a woman who could overwhelm me during a lunch hour. She consistently unloaded the sad state of affairs in her life plus informed me of my shortcomings as a friend. She would feel much better and I would be a wreck for two days. We don't do lunch anymore.

In John 10:10 Jesus says, "The thief comes only to steal and kill and destroy; I have come that they may have life, and have it to the full." Don't let the thief steal your joy. Accept God's offer of abundant life and pass His joy on to others. It may be difficult at first but God is much bigger than our bad habits.

Cherish all life from beginning to end.

For seventeen years I worked in a ministry serving women, their little ones and their families. God grew in me a deep love for His children. I thought that was my calling.

Then, WHOOPS, like slipping on ice, He moved me out when my mother died and my father needed daily care. God pulled me aside for two years to teach me about the other end of life. I entered a different world. Difficult but good. I learned to love and respect the elderly (even, maybe especially, cranky old guys).

Then, WHOOPS again. Dad died and along came my first grandson and the opportunity to care for him three mornings a week. Pure gift. Two heartbreaking miscarriages later our son, Matt, and daughter-in-law, Michele, gifted us with another precious grandson.

A year later Michele found a lump in her breast and life slipped again. A double mastectomy, the pain of chemotherapy, hair loss and a multitude of other difficult symptoms marked her journey. We couldn't walk the road for her but family and friends provided practical help, stability and love every step of the way. We walked the road with her and gradually courage and hope replaced fear and uncertainty. Michele's strength and incredible attitude buoyed the rest of us during this season. Another lesson—life is fragile and needs tender care in the middle, not just on either end.

Life is a long list of roller coaster highs and lows with plain old living in between. Be aware and cherish every minute of it. God is in it all and God is good. Let Him be your joy.

> *...the joy of the Lord is your strength.*
> Nehemiah 8:10

Learn to be content.

Examine your life and decide to be content with who you are and what you have. Now, I don't mean you shouldn't try to improve yourself or your situation if needed but you'll be a much more joy-filled person if you cultivate contentment in the process. In his book, *Holy Sweat*, Tim Hansel says, "We must be joyful now. Here...within...with who we are and what we've got." Good idea. Why is it so hard?

Human nature dangles a "grass is greener" carrot under our noses. Our culture tells us there is no such thing as too thin or too much stuff. The world we live in tells us our joy depends on how good we look, the status of our job, how much we accomplish and how many toys we possess. We are never taught enough is enough. Consequently, we go through life constantly looking around us and forever falling short. I don't know about guys but for us gals it's exhausting.

I have four sizes of clothing in my closet, a house that is never going to show up in the pages of *Better Homes and Gardens*, bad habits I battle, and pimples on top of my wrinkles. If all these imperfections were to disappear, would I suddenly find joy? No. I would find another list of things that aren't quite right, starting with my neck and upper arms.

So what do I do? Give up and let it all go? I don't think so.

I believe Paul nails the answer in Philippians 4:11-13, "...I have learned to be content in whatever circumstances I am. I know how to get along with humble means, and I also know how to live in prosperity; in any and every circumstance I have learned the secret of being filled and going hungry, both of having abundance and suffering need. I can do all things through Him who strengthens me" (NASB).

The fact that Paul says, "I have *learned* to be content..." tells me it wasn't always that way. He struggled too. He'd given up his status and privilege as a Pharisee to follow Christ. I'm sure contentment wasn't his first response to a wild storm at sea or the confinement of a filthy jail cell—but he learned and found joy in the middle of hardship, growth and change. We can too. Instead of trying so hard to get the things we think we *want*, let's take a look around and gratefully *want* what God gives us.

Until now you have not asked for anything in my name.
Ask and you will receive, and your joy will be complete.
John 16:24

What an incredible promise. In Jesus name, ask for the joy and freedom of contentment.

🎵 **Listen to music and sing.**

I hope I get a good singing voice when I get to Heaven. I sure don't have one now. I love to sing anyway. Singing lifts me out of myself as I dance around the kitchen praising God. I'm sure God doesn't care that I only have a range of five notes and those aren't always in quite the right key. He can't complain, it's the voice He gave me. He must love to hear me because He brings it up time and again:

Praise the LORD for the LORD is good;
Sing praise to his name, for that is pleasant.
Psalm 135:3

Worship the LORD with gladness;
Come before Him with joyful songs.
Psalm 100:2

Go ahead. Belt out some songs to the Lord. Read the Psalms and follow David's example of singing praise to God. You'll sound good to Him, your heart will rejoice and your soul will *feel*.

I like most music, not all but most. Music can lift up my soul, bring me to tears, touch places in my heart that need healing, and draw me closer to God. Music gets my toes tapping and my feet dancing, even if my partner is a five-year-old grandson. Music can speak to me in a way that few things can. As I lie on the couch and let classical music wash over me God ministers to my deepest longings, without words. The voice of an opera singer can bring a flood of tears and even though I don't understand Italian, I feel God tugging at my heart. My voice raised in a hymn with God's people on Sunday morning assures me all is well with my soul.

When life is hard and I feel distant from God, I need music.

When life is calm and simple and my heart full and thankful, I need to sing.

Sing joyfully to the LORD, you righteous;
It is fitting for the upright to praise him. Praise the LORD with the harp;
Make music to him on the ten-stringed lyre.
Sing to him a new song;
Play skillfully, and shout for joy.
Psalm 33:1-3

🎵 Turn on your light.

You are the world's light—a city on a hill, glowing in the night for all
to see. Don't hide your light! Let it shine for all; let your good deeds
glow for all to see, so that they will praise your heavenly Father.
Matthew 5:14-16 TLB

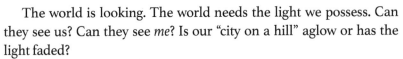

The world is looking. The world needs the light we possess. Can they see us? Can they see *me*? Is our "city on a hill" aglow or has the light faded?

When I was a new Christian, my little light was shining like crazy. I was overwhelmed by Jesus' love and sacrifice for my salvation. I didn't know much about being a Christian but I was sure excited. When asked why I was so happy, I would grin and say, "I'm a Christian now." I was probably annoyingly enthusiastic but my life changed dramatically and I wanted people to know.

Sadly, as time went by, I learned much more about being a Christian but my light didn't shine as bright. I loved and served the Lord and cherished Jesus and my faith, but I didn't sparkle anymore. Why? I had to really think about this. Here's what I came up with:

- ✦ I began to fear people's criticism of my enthusiasm and rejection of my faith, so I became more low-key and didn't share as often.
- ✦ I over-extended myself in service and grew tired and weary of the needs of others.
- ✦ I allowed sin to turn down the dimmer switch on my lamp.
- ✦ I became preoccupied with worries and lost the view from the hill.
- ✦ I began to keep Jesus at arms-length.
- ✦ I moved to the land of the negative and no longer reflected God's joy.
- ✦ I quit singing.

This list could be longer and I feel very uncomfortable as I think back. It's probably exactly how God wants me to feel. In Revelation 2:1-3 Jesus commends the church in Ephesus for their initial zeal and continued faithfulness and good works. Then in verse four He says,

Yet there is one thing wrong; you don't love me as at first! Think about those times of your first love (how different now!) and turn back to me again and work as you did before... TLB

I'm not in that pit anymore but I know how easy it is to fall in. Hmmm. I think I need to talk to God before I write any more. Be back in a bit.

✳ ✳ ✳

OK, I'm back. God didn't give me any stories to tell or thoughts to share. He gave me His Word:

> *Take care to live in me, and let me live in you.*
> *For a branch can't produce fruit when severed from the vine.*
> *Nor can you be fruitful apart from me.*
> *Yes, I am the Vine; you are the branches.*
> *Whoever lives in me and I in him shall produce a large crop of fruit.*
> *For apart from me you can't do a thing.*
> John 15:4-5 TLB

If your light has dimmed a bit, remember your first love, turn back and live as you did in the dawn of your faith. Let Jesus joy rekindle your light and His light rekindle your joy.

> *Restore to me the joy of your salvation and grant me*
> *a willing spirit to sustain me.*
> Psalm 51:12

Joy

Sharing Fruit

♫ Smile and laugh often.

I used to work with a young woman (a new employee) named Sherry who had a limited wardrobe but wore a beautiful smile. A single mom living on a modest income, Sherry's life wasn't easy. Her ex-husband proved flaky with the child support and her eleven-year-old son exhibited signs of becoming a teenager. Despite her circumstances, Sherry gave out smiles and cheerful words to everyone she met. No matter how I felt, Sherry would coax a return smile out of me as she passed my desk. She had a delightful laugh and the ability to send me into fits of giggles even if I was across the room and didn't know what she was laughing about. Sherry was also sweet and empathetic but it's her smile and laughter I remember.

The genuine smile, kind words and goofy laughter that drew everyone at work to Sherry proved contagious. We all smiled more and laughed with more ease. Sherry never laughed inappropriately or at someone else's expense and the rest of us followed her example. Petty differences seemed to melt away and we actually got more work done because we felt better. The whole mood of the office lifted. I wasn't nuts about that particular job but I looked forward to going to work because of the atmosphere Sherry created. I took my smile home with me at the end of the day.

I learned what a blessing it is to have someone look directly at me and smile. In that simple act I felt acknowledged and cheered and always smiled back. Then, while the warmth lingered, I gave the gift of a grin and maybe a pleasant greeting to the next person I met. It didn't cost me anything but I knew from experience how valuable a smile could be and, like looking in a mirror, it is almost always reflected back at me. Smiles and laughter show the world around us that there's a light on inside and God is at home in our heart.

A joyful heart makes a cheerful face...
Proverbs 15:13 NASB

Enjoy life so others can see and experience the joy of Jesus.

I am not a spontaneous person. This probably keeps me out of a lot of trouble but it also keeps me from experiencing much needed fun. An unexpected invitation to a dinner or an activity throws me off balance. I need to process the pros and cons before I commit. Where are the cons in going out to dinner? I'm not sure where this need to deliberate every decision comes from but I suspect it has something to do with being in control. I'm not the only one with this tendency.

"Would you like to go to the park?" I ask my five year old grandson.

"No," he answers flatly.

"OK," I answer looking out at the sunshine.

Not two minutes later he pipes up, "Grandma, help me find my shoes so we can go to the park."

He needed to think through this new information and when he felt comfortable and in control, he agreed. Part of this is his age but, I suspect he is a cautious soul like his grandma. There's nothing wrong with considering a new idea, it could be a bad one, just don't ponder too long or a great opportunity may pass you by.

I recently, without giving it any thought, hopped on a flimsy looking seat dangling from a heavy wire and whizzed off on a zip line headed straight for a huge tree. The brakes stopped me a few feet from death and I was so excited I couldn't wait to do it again. If I stopped to consider the possible consequences ahead of time, I never would have done it. Of course the brakes could have failed sending me crashing into the tree and I could be dead, but that's not how the adventure ended. Go for it.

The flip side of agreeing to spontaneous suggestions is to be the person who initiates the fun. You don't have to wait around for others to make your life interesting. Does a hike sound like fun? How about a coffee drink or an ice cream cone? Fly the idea by your family or pick up the phone and call a friend. The worst they can say is "no thanks." You can keep trying or go solo and enjoy your own company. The point is, you have the choice to be bored (there's really no excuse in God's fascinating world) or be willing to step out, sometimes of your comfort zone, and say "sure, I'd love to," even to yourself.

Our willingness to relax and enjoy the life God has given us demonstrates to others that being a Christian isn't super-sober or anti-fun. As Christians we are to glorify and praise God. Our joy in living and walking with Jesus should cause us to turn outward toward others. Perhaps they'll want to join us. Perhaps they'll begin to want Who we have.

How priceless is your unfailing love!
Both high and low among men
Find refuge in the shadow of your wings.
They feast on the abundance of your house;
You give them drink from your river of delights.
For with you is the fountain of life;
In your light we see light.
Psalm 36:7-9

🎵 Show joyful enthusiasm—it's catchy.

You will never be bored if you are excited about life and the people and world around you. Like ripples in a pond, your enthusiasm and joy will radiate from you and wash over the ankles of people wading in safe, shallow water.

Our next-door neighbors are enthusiastic people. Penny swims every morning, is an avid gardener, collects miniatures, enjoys decorating and creates beautiful colored pencil "paintings". She also accompanies Jeff on many of his adventures. Jeff loves astronomy and they frequently traipse off with their telescopes to star parties with other people in love with space.

Jeff and one of his sons are "Trekies" or Star Trek nuts for the less galactically informed. They go to conventions, collect memorabilia, and know every character.

Jeff and Penny love trains and roller coasters and movies. Jeff has owned a series of Corvettes that he takes to cruise-ins. The current one is metallic purple. You gotta love it. They travel and explore in a giant motor home. We participate by watering their plants and picking up their mail and newspaper.

We have been friends and neighbors for thirty-nine years and are witness to their enthusiasm and joy. Do they see the same thing in us? We have different interests and priorities but Rich and I are commanded to,

...Love the LORD your God with all your heart, and with all your soul,
and with all your mind, and with all your strength...and you shall love
your neighbor as yourself.
Mark 12:30-31 NASB

Are we living out God's plan with enthusiasm and joy?

Our friends opened our eyes. We possess different temperaments so our enthusiasm won't look the same. Rich and I are not total duds but we're quieter and not as adventurous. We've decided to ask God to help us deepen our focus and enjoyment in our faith, our church, our kids and grandsons, our hobbies, our friends, our marriage and our world. We want to be interested and interesting. We want others to see our love and enthusiasm for the Lord Jesus and the joy-filled life He has given us.

We may even need to find someone to pick up the mail and feed the cats. Jeff and Penny can't do it, they won't be home. "See, ya!"

The LORD has done great things for us; and we are filled with joy.
Psalm 126:3

🎵 Make the most of every day and let others in on your joy.

Each day is a gift, an adventure, a miracle!

These are not my first thoughts when the alarm goes off in the morning. I do not leap from my cozy covers and bound off to explore what God has prepared for me. No, no. I roll out of bed, locate my glasses the cat knocked off the nightstand, and shuffle toward the bathroom. A cursory glance in the mirror tells me I have a lot of work to do.

Sometime during my second cup of coffee I begin to perk up. Yes, the Lord has made this day and given it to me to live. Cool. Sleep to sleep, a little lifetime packed into twenty-four hours. Now I'm getting into it. I may have my day planned. Maybe lunch with the girls (good) maybe a root canal (not so good). It really doesn't matter. God has made His own plans and I need to get moving in anticipation of what He has in store for me.

What can I do today to help someone else enjoy their day? Who needs encouragement? Who needs laughter? Who needs a hug or pat on the back? God has so many treasures hidden away in this day. He wants me to discover them and share the wealth.

I need to pay attention to all the things He wants me to do and see. All the people He wants me to meet. All the thoughts and feelings He wants me to experience. All the joy He wants me to share. There is so much out there. TODAY!

This is the day which the Lord has made; let us rejoice and be glad in it.
Psalm 118:24 NASB

🎵 **Sing, whistle, hum...someone may hear Jesus.**

I wrote earlier about the importance of music and singing in nurturing joy in my life. Now I need to give it away.

Stopped behind a young woman at a red light one morning, my eyes were drawn to a lot of movement in the front seat. I don't know what she was listening to but she swayed and waved her hands like a band leader. I caught an occasional glimpse of her face as it passed the rearview mirror and her mouth was moving quite enthusiastically. I laughed until my eyes watered.

The light changed and she headed off into her day. I wiped my eyes and headed into mine. Nothing extraordinary took place except a sixty-second peek into the world of an unselfconscious fellow driver. A normal workday commute but I laughed and sang my way through the rest of my day. My fellow driver provided a delightful reminder to enjoy other people as they sing to their music. Mine is not the only song.

I used to make sure no other drivers were close by before singing in the car. How uptight and buttoned-down! Now I sing with abandon and if I catch someone looking I just smile without missing a beat. I may look foolish but if the guy in the next lane gets a laugh, great. If he pops in a CD and sings out for all to see, the music may just catch on. We each sing different songs on different days. We know a variety of tunes in endless rhymes and rhythms. We open our mouths and voices as unique as snowflakes burst forth. It doesn't matter how we sound, this old world needs to see and hear us open our hearts and sing.

A word of caution. If you have children you will be a total embarrassment to them. They will slump in their seat below window level and moan, "Motheeeeeerrrrr." If you are a public hummer, whistler, or singer, like my mother, your offspring will be mortified. However, chances are they will catch and carry the tune down the road into their own lives.

Many of us spend much of our time at work or home isolated from one another by physical or emotional walls or maybe by our machines and gadgets. Sometimes we simply spend too much time living inside our own heads. An occasional intrusion into each other's space through song, without requirements or participation, helps us remember we are not alone.

I watched a video recently about a "flash mob" of singers at a crowded mall at Christmas. Dressed in ordinary clothes, some carrying packages, first one person, then another began singing the Hallelujah Chorus. Soon more and more singers, scattered throughout the crowd joined in until the entire choir filled the air with song. Everyone stopped, surprised at first then smiling, even crying, as they realized what was happening. Some joined in but most just listened in awe. For a few minutes the shopping frenzy ceased and people looked at each other and smiled as the music connected them and touched something in their hearts. When the song ended, the singers blended back into the crowd to the sound of cheering and applause. The video I watched on You Tube has been viewed over fifty-one million times. We need more of that.

There are so many hurting people, so many souls who have stepped away from God and are aching to hear from Him. Joyous or gentle, always sensitive, a hum a whistle or a song—your music may provide the melody the Holy Spirit chooses to flood His joy and *Amazing Grace* into another heart, including yours.

But let all who take refuge in you be glad; let them ever sing for joy.
Psalm 5:11

FRUIT FOR THOUGHT

Joy

Nurturing Fruit

1. What keeps you from experiencing joy in your life? How could you choose joy in spite of your circumstances?

2. Do you or someone close to you have a habit of grumbling and complaining? What specific consequences do you see from this behavior? You can't change others but is there any "grumbling or disputing" in your own life? How might you begin to acknowledge and overcome this?

3. Have you experienced the importance of cherishing every season of life? If you haven't thought this through, visit the neonatal unit at a children's hospital, volunteer to drive someone to their chemotherapy appointment or spend an afternoon visiting the residents of a nursing home. You may begin to see the world through God's eyes. What is your reaction to this suggestion?

4. In what ways do you struggle with contentment? How does your culture make this difficult for you personally?

5. Have you ever experienced spiritual doldrums? If so, what were your symptoms? Is your light still dim or are you back on the hill shining again (or maybe somewhere in between?) Reach out your hand to receive or give help and encouragement. We have all been spiritually low at some point in our lives and we need each other.

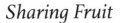

Sharing Fruit

1. How do your smiles and laughter impact the world you live in, especially the people closest to you?

2. Are you able to enjoy life so others can see being a Christian isn't super-sober or anti-fun? If not, what steps can you take to begin to experience and display the joy of the Lord?

3. What are you enthusiastic about? Does your enthusiasm inspire the world around you?

4. What can you do today to bring joy into someone else's life? List three action steps.

5. What role does music and singing have in your life? Are you willing to make a little music within the hearing of others? Being sensitive to your situation, how might your music touch people for God?

❄ ❄ ❄

Grab your notebook and write out...

- One Scripture from this chapter that is particularly meaningful to you.
- Your Thoughts and Stories

❄ ❄ ❄

Chapter Three

THE FRUIT OF THE SPIRIT IS ... PEACE

Mary Ann

A purple velvet loveseat enveloped Rich and me as we waited for a table at the Spaghetti Factory. We turned as a gust of cold air blew in through the ornate front doors along with a group of elderly ladies. They were nicely dressed with lovely silver hairdos. It appeared they hadn't seen each other for a while and it was fun to watch as they hugged and chatted. One lady in particular caught my attention. We met long ago at a Bible study when I was a new Christian and her laughter and peaceful, welcoming spirit helped me relax and join in.

She looked like the other ladies except her face glowed. That probably sounds corny, but when she wasn't actually smiling—when her face relaxed—she maintained a beautiful "almost smile" look. Her eyes twinkled and she looked like she was interested in everything going on around her. I remembered how much I liked this lady. I remembered how much she loved the Lord. I poked Rich so he would notice.

"See that woman with the red sweater. Her name is MaryAnn and she went to Joy in the Morning Bible study when I was there. I want to look like her."

"Fine, but would you mind waiting a few years?"

"Sarcasm is a terrible thing. Look at the expression on her face, you know what I mean, she looks, I don't know, at peace with herself."

He just smiled.

I walked over to the group and tapped MaryAnn on the shoulder. She turned and grinned when she recognized me.

"Annie. What a nice surprise. Let me introduce you to my friends."

She had something nice to say about each of the ladies and introduced me as the "delightful, *young* woman" she met at a Bible study (I *was* young when we met). I felt great.

Introductions over, we exchanged e-mail addresses and promised to get caught up.

"I don't think we had e-mail when we first met, did we?" she asked, laughing.

"No." I said. "It's been a long time. I'm glad we ran into each other."

"Me, too." MaryAnn reached out and squeezed my hand.

The hostess seated us and I didn't see MaryAnn again until we lapped up our spumoni ice cream and got up to leave. As we passed her table I took a peek and there she sat, listening intently to another lady. Her eyes sparkled and a smile played around the corners of her mouth. She made a positive impression on me and I was just a nosey, long-ago friend. I didn't notice her wrinkles. I don't remember if she was chubby or thin. I just saw that lovely face radiating interest, humor and an underlying peace.

MaryAnn made me smile. She caused me to think. She looked like what I thought a Christian *should* look like—she was lit from within.

I know MaryAnn experienced her share of troubles. We grieved with her when she lost her husband to cancer when we were in Bible study together. Her teenage daughters were being teenagers. Mary Ann faced financial problems and her own health concerns. She probably possessed a list of difficulties I know nothing of. We all have a list.

Mary Ann could have chosen to wallow in her heartache and problems. Instead, she chose to rise above the very real struggles in her life and live out Colossians 3:15, "Let the peace of Christ rule in your hearts, since as members of one body you were called to peace. And be thankful."

I've done a lot of wallowing, making myself and those around me miserable. Have you? I think I'll try giving God my list of woes, draw closer to Him, and ask Him to "rule in my heart." If Mary Ann's face and words and actions could reflect the peace of God, so can ours.

Peace

Nurturing Fruit

 Simplify your life to make room for peace.

I used to feel guilty if I didn't zip around in an attempt to accomplish several things at once. Sit down and read? Play a game with a child? Go for a walk with my husband? Aggggh! So many other things screamed for my attention. Really? Like what?

The dishwasher, grocery store, laundry, phone calls, career, church, dust, the daily question, "what's for dinner?"—all the to-do's of life. The list is endless and will keep you stuck like a hamster on her wheel unless you jump off. Yes, those things need doing but are they more important than the simple things and the people we miss as we fly by? No.

One of my biggest regrets as I look back on my life from my current position as a grandma is lack of balance between my to-do list and my family. I said "yes" to projects on other people's agendas. I worked too hard to keep a tidy house (with two little boys!) in case someone should stop by. I wore myself out as I tried to keep up with too many commitments that didn't matter or could have been done by someone else. Irritable and tired I short-changed my family and myself.

I don't get a "do-over" but I can make some changes so I enjoy life more, and have fewer regrets when it's time to go.

- I need to pace myself and spread projects and activities out over time to reserve space for God, others and myself.
- Say "no" more often and with less guilt. This is easier said than done, so practice. I need to remind myself that "No" is a complete sentence. I don't need to add an excuse. If I must feel guilty, I practice "short-term guilt"—five minutes max. If I choose to say "Yes," there will be less room for something else. Make sure your "yes" is worth it.
- Allow extra time to do things and get places. Take some of the "rush" out of life. I keep a book or magazine in the car in case I'm early.
- Take one day at a time. I worry too much about what tomorrow may bring. What a waste. Live today and cherish what God puts before me. Today is my life. I know this is a cliché but it is scriptural:

Teach us to number our days and recognize how few they are;
help us to spend them as we should.
Psalm 90:12 TLB

 Choose to be satisfied and peace will follow.

Let's see, what messes with my satisfaction level?

- Stuff. Let's face it—we can't have everything. Where on earth would we put it? I spent many years in "stuff" acquisition. Plus, I've inherited other people's possessions. I used to long for more. Now I realize I have everything I need and then some. Don't get me wrong, I do love my "stuff" but it's no longer where my heart is. I haven't quite embraced the "less is more" concept but I'm working on it.
- House. It's been a long struggle but I've finally come to love my 1970's house with the popcorn ceilings. Rich and I used to spend every Sunday after church going to open houses in

search of the "perfect" house. The houses we wanted were too expensive and the ones we could afford were just like the one we already owned. One Sunday we pulled into our driveway and realized how good it felt to be home. We had found our perfect house.

♦ Money. Rich and I have gotten ourselves in over our heads several times in our forty-five years of marriage. We're not big spenders we just never made tons of money. More than once we've maxed out our credit card so that any extra money we earned needed to head in that direction. We eventually got them paid off and now try to be "cash and carry" people like our parents. However, life was stressful as we learned this lesson and I think credit cards and the American tendency to live beyond our means is a huge contributor to family stress and the divorce rate. No, Rich and I are not getting divorced but we can see how easily money can trip up a marriage.

♦ Myself. As I've gotten older I've become a bit fluffy (twenty pounds of fluff to be exact). I'm rarely happy with my hair or my weight, my clothes are boring, I have great intentions but bad follow-through...you get the picture. I'm never satisfied.

I know God wants me to grow and change in my journey toward Christ-likeness. I can't just give up and give in. I also think He wants me to enjoy the trip and who I am along the way. So, I'll move forward (even if it means baby steps) to change the things I can, and allow God to handle the rest. Change doesn't happen overnight which is why I usually give up. I'm praying for a satisfied heart in the midst of commitment to follow God's lead.

The Lord is my shepherd, I shall not be in want.
He makes me lie down in green pastures,
he leads me beside quiet waters, he restores my soul.
He guides me in paths of righteousness for his name's sake.
Psalm 23:1-3

Have a grateful heart.

I began keeping a "Gratitude Journal" a couple of years ago after reading, *One Thousand Gifts* by Ann Voskamp. The daily habit of writing down God's blessings has been one of the most useful and pleasant disciplines I have undertaken since becoming a Christian and one I've actually stuck with—most of the time. I usually journal and write in a spiral notebook but for the Gratitude Journal I splurged on a pretty spiral bound journal (I hate trying to write in a bound book—it's a battle). Every day, usually in the morning, I jot down things I am grateful for—from the amazing to the mundane. Sometimes I write long paragraphs, other times I'm in a bullet point mood. It doesn't matter. I find the fewer rules I place on myself the more apt I am to follow through. I do date every entry, though, so when I look back in the book I know where I was in the scheme of things. This often triggers other memories of that particular time or place.

My Gratitude Journal has helped me to:

* Think about and be aware of my days rather than bounce through them from one thing on my "to do" list to the next.
* Look for and appreciate the multitude of blessings God pours into my life every day. I pretend I'm looking through a camera lens, focus and "click" take a written picture.
* Face difficulties with a little less stress—more peace. I began to realize that God blesses me even in the middle of a mess, and most messes don't last forever.
* I have begun to see the world with fresh eyes, sense God's love in a very personal way and trust Him with my future without fear or boundaries.

This is the very day God acted—let's celebrate and be festive.
Psalm 118:24 MSG

 Build some "peace time" into your day.

Life can be hectic and I often jump into my day feet first and running. I got in the habit long ago, because I was working full time, of getting up at least an hour and a half before I had to leave so I had plenty of time to get ready, drink my coffee, eat my almond butter toast, and spend time reading my Bible or a devotional and praying. I was usually the only one up and I came to treasure this time.

Now my schedule is a little looser but I still get up early to connect with God before I'm "into" the day. This is often the only quiet space I have for God to speak to me. Actually, I'm sure He's speaking to me all the time but the early morning is when I focus and *listen* without distractions. The silence before God is a precious introduction to my busy days.

Our schedules and body clocks may be different but we all need time every day to pay attention to the Holy Spirit and allow Him to speak to our hearts and minds. If we take time to soak up the Lord like a solar lamp soaks up the sun, we can't help but give out the light we've taken in. When we choose to be deliberate in our time and place to be alone with God, He will be faithful to meet us there. If we expect to meet God, we are more likely to keep the appointment!

My soul waits in silence for God only;
From Him is my salvation, He only is my rock and my salvation,
My stronghold; I shall not be greatly shaken.
Psalm 62:1-2 NASB

🍎 Don't worry.

Worry is a waste of time, steals your peace, and casts a shadow on those around you. Easy to say—hard to do—especially if you have children or happen to watch the news. Our "self" wants to control things and we become anxious and frustrated when we can't. What we *can* do is pray, *do* what we are able, and *release* the rest into God's capable hands. Worry and trust don't blend well together and God wants us to trust Him so He can give us His peace.

I have spent untold hours and sleepless nights pondering worst case scenarios which never came to pass. I recently had a small lump in my throat. I had to wait a week before seeing the ear, nose and throat doctor. During that time I worried and lay awake at night planning my memorial service. It turned out to be nothing serious. I wasted a perfectly good week, threw my peace out the window, and completely failed to trust God with the unknowns in my life. However, since it appeared I would live a bit longer, I decided to ask for a hearing test—just as a baseline. I will soon be coughing up money for hearing aids. If my ears worked, I would probably hear God chuckle and say, "Surprise! Didn't think to worry about that, did you?"

When something serious or out of the ordinary happens, it's almost always a surprise. No previous worry, but I do tend to be taken aback. Now I've got myself thinking maybe I'm missing something I should be chewing on—there goes my peace again. What a silly woman! It takes a conscious choice on my part to relinquish my thoughts of gloom and doom and trust God with the big picture. I easily become overwhelmed when circumstances are beyond my control but I am learning to let go of anxious thoughts, do what I can, and let God be God.

In the meantime, I will trust God and let Him replace my worry with His peace.

You will keep in perfect peace him whose mind is steadfast,
because he trusts in you.
Isaiah 26:3

From personal experience I know Celebrate Recovery and ALA-NON meetings always include a portion of the "Serenity Prayer." This is probably true for most recovery programs. I'm sure you're familiar with this poem but it's worth internalizing regarding peace.

God grant me the serenity
To accept the things I cannot change;
courage to change the things I can;
and wisdom to know the difference.
Living one day at a time;
Enjoying one moment at a time;
Accepting hardships as the pathway to peace;

Taking, as He did, this sinful world
as it is, not as I would have it;
Trusting that He will make all things right
If I surrender to His Will;
That I may be reasonably happy in this life
and supremely happy with Him
Forever in the next.
Amen.

—Reinhold Niebuhr

Peace

Sharing Fruit

 Wear a peaceful face.

Be aware of what your face is doing in its "down time." The next time you're sitting at a red light, look at the faces of the drivers passing in front of you. What a morose looking bunch of people. Or the passengers on a bus. Most of them look like they're headed for prison or, worse yet, the line at DMV. I'm pretty sure the majority of these people aren't as miserable as they look, they're just unaware of their faces. If you're like me, your face probably doesn't look much different from theirs. However, if you spot someone laughing or looking happy or unselfconsciously singing to the radio in the car, it makes you grin. Then someone sees your expression and on it goes. I don't know how many times my spirits have been lifted simply by the light coming off another person.

I just checked out my face in the bathroom mirror. Hmmm...when I relax my face I look crabby. Not good. Well, maybe its age related and can't be helped. Looking back, though, I remember Rich and the boys occasionally asking me if I was okay.

"Mom, are you mad?"

"Honey, are you upset about something?"

I was usually fine. I just *looked* grouchy or unhappy. I *did not* look at peace with myself or anyone around me. So this isn't an age related condition. I'm just generally unaware of what my face is doing when it's not busy doing something else. No matter how carefully applied my make-up may be, it doesn't matter much if I wear an unpleasant expression underneath.

Now, I'm not saying we should walk around all the time looking like we've paid for an over-enthusiastic face lift or that we can never relax. I am saying, however, it wouldn't kill us, as Christians, to cultivate a pleasant look and wear it as much as possible. We need to develop a look that says we're enjoying ourselves, we're interested, compassionate and approachable. A look that shows people we have a relationship with the incredible God of the universe who fills us with His peace and joy.

Of course there are times when our feelings or our problems make it very difficult for us to function at all let alone muster up inner peace and a friendly expression. I'm not encouraging us to wear masks to hide our feelings, but I am suggesting we make a conscious choice to let our relationship with Jesus show on our faces. It will come across in our attitudes. It may even perk us up and tweak our perspective on our circumstances. What's more, it can have the same effect on others. It did on me. Remember Mary Ann?

Now go look in a mirror and smile big. Relax your smile without relaxing the rest of your face. You look like you have a very pleasant secret, don't you? Wear the expression around the house for a while. Get used to the feeling. See if your family notices. (Trick: if you pull your ears up and back, the rest of your face will snap up with them. An instant facelift.) I didn't do any kind of a study on this so I asked Rich to try. His ears never moved, but he looks nice anyway. I guess it doesn't work for everyone but it's worth a try.

Now, take your peaceful face out in public. Start with the grocery store. Keep it on while you're driving, there are big windows in that car! Remember, your countenance is showing. You never know who may be looking and, before you know it, you'll see the same look reflected back to you from other faces.

Just as water mirrors your face, so your face mirrors your heart."
Proverbs 27:19 MSG

 Avoid being quarrelsome (don't disturb the peace).

We all know someone (hopefully not ourselves) who will argue about anything.

- Say it's a nice day and they can give you five reasons why it isn't.
- They ask a question and, before you can answer, begin stating their opinion over the top of you (usually upping the volume).
- Make an innocent comment and they deliberately misunderstand and become angry or cry. I'm not sure which is worse.

These people are exhausting and, if you possibly can, you soon learn to avoid them. If you live or work with them, you emotionally withdraw.

We also all know people who enjoy others and have a positive outlook on life.

- Say it's a nice day and they have five reasons why they agree with you.
- They are good listeners and make an effort to really hear what you are saying.
- Make an innocent comment and they ask questions to draw you into grace-filled conversation.
- They have a very long fuse and rarely become angry.

God loves quarrelsome people as much as anyone else, but He would prefer we not be one of them. If you see yourself in the first list, it may be time to prayerfully ask the Holy Spirit to settle His peace upon your heart.

...Everyone should be quick to listen, slow to speak and slow to become angry...
James 1:19

 Give it to God so He can grant you the peace to give to others.

Surrender is a hard word for most of us. We hang on to our worries and fears and stuff as if they were worth something—they're not. They simply lock us in a cage when God would have us free. This world is a hard place to take up God's challenge to let go—but if we are to have real peace and be God's fruit-bearers, we need to pry our fingers loose from whatever it is we hold so tightly.

Rich's Aunt Gertrude died about twenty years ago. He was the executor of the estate. Once her apartment was cleaned out and the family had chosen the things they wanted we held a garage sale at our house. All the things that didn't sell, mainly clothes and miscellaneous old stuff, we hauled up to the bedroom recently vacated when our oldest son left for college.

Now, I had a house full of our own possessions but I was constantly drawn to that room full of *more*. There was nothing there I needed. Aunt Gertrude's clothes were outdated and the wrong size and the left-over dishes and decorative items wouldn't work in our house. I knew it all needed to go but I couldn't stay out of that room. Sort of like when you stare into the refrigerator hoping you missed some wonderful goodie the last time you looked but it's never there.

I was finally released from the room's gravitational pull when Matt came home from college for the summer.

"Mom," he yelled from what used to be his bedroom. "There's nowhere for me to sleep. What is all this junk?"

"Well..." I didn't have a good answer.

The next day it was gone and, you know what? I felt free. I had been weighed down because I wouldn't let go of things I didn't even need or want. I learned a valuable lesson as I shifted my focus from things to people. God blessed me with tremendous peace when I opened my grasping hands, left all that stuff behind, and began to

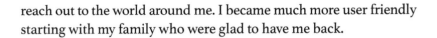

reach out to the world around me. I became much more user friendly starting with my family who were glad to have me back.

> *Peace I leave with you; my peace I give you. I do not give*
> *to you as the world gives.*
> *Do not let your hearts be troubled and do not be afraid.*
> John 14:27

🍑 Remain calm and calm others.

During our forty-five years of marriage Rich and I have experienced our share of family crises and even heartbreak. We both have a role to play in these situations.

I have two settings. I either attempt to take control and fix the problem (regardless of whether or not I know what's going on) or I panic and resort to my *"Chicken Little and the Sky is Falling"* routine. Neither action is helpful, they simply add annoyance and confusion.

Rich, on the other hand, is the embodiment of the statement, "keep calm and carry on." He doesn't panic but calmly does what needs doing. When the boys were younger and threw up, he would clean them up and swamp up the mess while I was outside gulping fresh air.

During really hard times Rich goes into action but relies on God to lead the way. Regardless of the seriousness of the situation or the emotional pain he is feeling he trusts God with the process and the outcome. The side-effect of his faith and dependence on God is that everyone else settles down and is either reassured, comforted, strengthened to help...whatever is needed. He has pulled my chicken-self out from under chunks of sky more times that I can count so I can release my knee-jerk reactions, turn to God and be helpful (or at least get out of the way).

I'm doing better as I get older. My husband's example has led me into a deeper trust in God, a "no matter what" kind of trust. Sometimes I still react like the sky is falling but I'm getting better.

Like a pebble dropped in a pond, the peace of God extends out from us in concentric circles gently washing over the lives He wants to touch.

*But the wisdom from above is first pure, then peaceable, gentle, reason-
able, full of mercy and good fruits, unwavering, without hypocrisy.
And the seed whose fruit is righteousness is sown in peace
by those who make peace.*
James 3:17-18 NASB

 Stir peace into battered relationships.

A friend shared this story with me (I changed the names).

Mary and Jennifer were acquaintances on the way to becoming
good friends. They shared many things in common and enjoyed
each other's company.

The bubble burst when they signed up for the same planning
committee at their children's school. They both had strong opinions
about school policies and curriculum. Unfortunately, they rarely
agreed. Jennifer was out-spoken and Mary was quiet but her body
language and occasional tone of voice spoke volumes.

This behavior intensified through several meetings as the rest of
the group became more and more uncomfortable. Very little was accomplished and Jennifer and Mary were no longer on their way to
becoming good friends.

Finally, Mandy, the group leader, took control. She asked Mary
and Jennifer to come early to the next meeting. When they arrived,
she sat them down and described their negative behavior and how it
created a stressful atmosphere in which no one felt safe and nothing
was being accomplished. Then she looked at each of them and said,
"Knock it off. Work out your differences and behave like grown wom-
en or find somewhere else to serve. Separately."

Jennifer and Mary looked at each other. After a guilty pause they
each admitted to their stubbornness and pride and asked forgiveness.
When the rest of the group arrived they told them how sorry they were
for being so disruptive and promised to change their ways. Everyone
relaxed, they were forgiven and future meetings ran smoothly.

Jennifer and Mary *did* become very good friends. God planted
the original seeds of their friendship. He gave each of them the love
and grace to face their stubborn pride, ride out the storm in their

relationship and remain standing. They both embraced God's call to peace and are stronger now because they still have each other.

If it is possible, as far as it depends on you, live at peace with everyone.
Romans 12:18

Finally, brethren, rejoice, be made complete, be comforted, be like-minded, live in peace; and the God of love and peace shall be with you.
2 Corinthians 13:11 (NASB)

FRUIT FOR THOUGHT

Peace

Nurturing Fruit

1. List three ways to simplify your life to embrace God's peace. How will this touch the lives of people close to you?

2. What messes with your sense of peace?

3. If you aren't currently keeping a Gratitude Journal, try it. Keep it simple, three things a day for starters. How does this affect your peace with God and others?

4. Can you think of one way to build some "peace time" into your day?

5. How does worry affect your sense of peace? List three things from the past you have worried about that never happened. Does worry demonstrate trust in God? Why?

Sharing Fruit

1. Has your life been touched by God's peace shining through another person? If so, what were the qualities or actions that had a positive effect on you? Is there one quality you would like to try to incorporate into your life? Did you try the pleasant face test? Could you see a difference? Did anyone notice?

2. Have you spent time with a habitually quarrelsome person? How did that affect your peace? If you see yourself as the offender, what steps can you take to change your ways?

3. Is there something disturbing your peace? Something you are holding onto you know you need to surrender to God but can't seem to let go of? Take a close look at your life (where you've been, where you are, and where you want to be). Ask God to help you surrender the empty promises of the world for the peace that only He can give. How would this change your attitude and behavior toward the people in your world?

4. Do you identify with "calm" Rich or "Chicken Little" Annie? Explain your answer. If you have a tendency to see the sky falling, how does this effect your peace and that of those around you?

5. Are there any relationships in your life that need mending? Are you willing to do your part to reconcile and restore peace?

Grab your notebook and write out...

♦ One Scripture from this chapter that is particularly meaningful to you.

♦ Your Thoughts and Stories

Chapter Four

THE FRUIT OF THE SPIRIT IS ... PATIENCE

Rosie

A blur of blonde curls and pink overalls headed for the "down" escalator at the mall. I ran toward her thinking, "she's headed for a fall."

Suddenly she stopped—just short of the first step. Now I could see she wore a halter with a leash attached. Her watchful mother held the other end.

After relief, my first reaction was, "That's awful. The poor kid's not a dog. Her mother should hold her so she can't get so close to danger."

As I watched, the toddler walked over and lifted her arms to be picked up. I think she scared herself. Mama walked her to the escalator and firmly explained how Rosie could get hurt. I wish I could say I would have shown such restrain with my own boys. I wouldn't even take them to the mall by myself. Patience wasn't my strong suit.

We were all headed into Macy's so I got to witness Rosie as an open jewelry display caught her eye. She wriggled out of her Mom's arms and off she went, but only so far, stopped before she could pull the shelf of sparklies over on herself. This made her mad. She wanted that jewelry and showed signs of a full-blown tantrum. Mom stooped to eye level. "Rosie, I know the bracelets are pretty but they're not

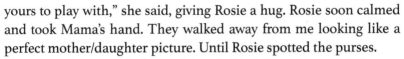

yours to play with," she said, giving Rosie a hug. Rosie soon calmed and took Mama's hand. They walked away from me looking like a perfect mother/daughter picture. Until Rosie spotted the purses.

"Purses for Rosie," she exclaimed gleefully as she yanked away and headed for the end of her tether. Mom reeled her in and, with a touch of sternness in her voice this time, explained the need to stay close. Mom let this concept sink in for a moment before saying,

"Let's go to the little girl's part of the store and see if we can find a purse that's just right for you."

Rosie lit up. "Can we Mommy?"

I was tempted to follow them to the children's department, expecting a good show, but needed to get home. Rosie's entertaining behavior caused me to change my mind about the leash. Rosie didn't need to be carried. She needed freedom to explore and experience her world in the presence of someone who would lovingly and patiently help her learn about boundaries and obedience.

As I walked to my car, I had to smile. Just that morning I read Psalm 37 and underlined verses 23 and 24. "The steps of a man are established by the LORD; and He delights in his way. When he falls, he shall not be hurled headlong; because the LORD is the One who holds his hand" (NASB).

Lord, You have such creative ways of reminding me of our relationship.

Just as Rosie is attached to her mother, I am attached to You. Like Rosie's mom, You love me and give me my freedom—up to a point. I often choose to wander close to temptation before I feel the tug back to the safety of Your arms.

Sometimes, though, I ignore the tug and stretch the tether to its limit and get into trouble. But You don't leave me there. You lift me up, dust me off, and help me deal with the consequences of my choices. Your patience and forgiveness calm my rebellious, wandering heart. You explain—sometimes gently, sometimes sternly—how important it is to obey you. Off we go until I forget my last experience and run off after something else. I'm not much different from Rosie—just older.

Lord, I'm very grateful that You don't allow me to be "hurled headlong" when I stumble in my walk with You. Teach me to stay close. To hold tight to the safety of Your hand. Help me extend to others the endless patience and grace You extend to me. Help me focus my eyes on Jesus and delight my heart in the wonders of my Savior who chose the cross to demonstrate His longsuffering love, endless forgiveness and patient entreaty for my soul.

Patience

Nurturing Fruit

 Slow down—patience is waiting.

This is very hard for me. I walk fast, talk fast, fling my arms around, and eat fast. I type fast with lots of errors. It's hard for me to settle down. The problem is I feel productive but I'm not always focused on the right goal. What's that saying? "I don't know where I'm going but I'm making great time." That's me.

I often zip through my devotionals and Bible reading in the morning—check. Shower, make-up, hair and clothes—check. Ignore beeping phone—check. Housework and grocery shopping—check. Swing by the church to turn in receipts for ministry supplies—check. Fix dinner and feed husband—check. Watch a little TV, wash off make-up and finally read my e-mail and listen to phone messages. I find I missed an invitation to lunch from an out-of-town friend and an opportunity to visit with a hurting woman from church. An urgent prayer request from the prayer chain was posted at 9:00 a.m. I could still pray but missed the immediate need. I also remember that when Rich retold his round of golf, I was folding laundry and didn't pay much attention. My drive to accomplish my "to do" list and my impatience with anything that might slow me down had cost me dearly.

This is how I patterned my days for a long time, until grandchildren. These adorable boys force me to slow down and pay attention. Instead of flying through my time with them, I sit on the floor and play cars, read stories, share sticky sandwiches and play hide and seek with my five-year-old Garrison. I root for my ten-year-old, Emitt, at football and baseball and basketball games and help with homework (we're both struggling with fractions). We cook together, watch TV together, and eat French fries dripping in catsup. I slow down and focus—I don't want to miss a thing. I am patient with them and their little boy ways and patient with myself as I let go of the unimportant.

Slowly, I'm beginning to shift the focus of my days. I heard a wonderful saying, "The person in front of you is almost always more important than the task at hand." I've lived it backwards for a long time. Now I want to savor my moments with God, my husband, my friends, my family and myself. I want David's words to be true of me.

O LORD, my heart is not proud, nor my eyes, haughty; nor do I involve myself in great matters, or in things too difficult for me. Surely I have composed and quieted my soul; like a weaned child rests against his mother, my soul is like a weaned child within me.
Psalm 131:1-2 NASB

I'm asking God to quiet my restless heart, remind me how patiently He deals with me and help me let go of my impatient speed so I can embrace the people He puts in front of me.

Be patient without complaining or playing the victim.

Patience for the Christian means exhibiting the Fruit of the Spirit when we are faced with difficult people, challenged by circumstances, tired, sick, struggling with our hormones, or facing personal problems—with steadfastness, joy and thanksgiving. Of course, God does not expect us to tolerate abuse or bad behavior but it is patience with love, joy and thanksgiving that make Christians look different from the rest of the world. This is a tall order.

Patience with difficult people and circumstances can be a real challenge. God and I are working on this. My favorite impatient behavior is the "sigh." Anything that poses an inconvenience or mild irritation can bring on the intake of breath and the audible exhale. I do this so often I'm hardly aware of it anymore so God brought it to my attention through fellow "sighers" at the post office.

I was second in line to mail a small package. The man in front of me juggled a twenty piece bulk mail order. I could have left but a large, creatively wrapped package intrigued me. A cut-off vacuum cleaner box on the bottom haphazardly taped to a smaller disposable diaper box. The mysterious contents appeared heavy as the man strained to shove it along with his hip. I wanted to see if it would be accepted.

Now, our local post office is quite small with only one woman behind the counter—ever. If you go there and see a line, you know no one is going to open another window—ever. Ten minutes into my wait a man came in and got in line behind me. A short time later a woman arrived. First, the man sighed quite audibly (if no one hears you, what's the point?) Then the woman sighed and grumbled about inconsiderate people who take too much time with big mailings. The man sighed again, the woman continued to grumble. The fellow with the order began to shift from foot to foot, looking over his shoulder uncomfortably.

The two behind me got louder and louder until the clerk stopped what she was doing, glared at the complainers and said, "I'm the only one here and this gentleman is well within the hours for bulk mail. If you can't quietly wait your turn, you're welcome to come back later." They glared back, sighed again, turned and left. Quite a show. The man ahead of me relaxed, his crazy package was accepted, and I decided to remove sighing and grumbling from my repertoire. My husband said I should mention this is a work in progress.

Then there's the victim. Being of a certain age (okay, post-menopausal) I often let my patience level be determined by my feelings. In other words, I frequently have no patience. I know my short-temper and shorter fuse are not in God's plan for me but I consider my behavior perfectly justified because it's how I *feel*. Of course, I'm allowed my feelings but when they spill over onto everyone in my path with impatience and snappiness I need to bite my tongue, pray hard and lay low until I can behave like a composed, Spirit-filled woman instead of an inconsiderate old brat.

We are all faced with difficult circumstances throughout our lives. It's during struggles that we learn and grow. Sometimes I would just as soon not learn and grow but God has other plans.

...be filled with the knowledge of His will in all spiritual wisdom and understanding, so that you may walk in a manner worthy of the Lord, to please Him in all respects, bearing fruit in every good work and increasing in the knowledge of God; strengthened with all power, according to His glorious steadfastness and patience, joyously giving thanks to the Father, who has qualified us to share in the inheritance of the saints in light.
Colossians 1:9-12 NASB

 Wait patiently for God's next move.

I chose the story of Rosie for a reason. I identify with her. I don't wait well and patience depends on my willingness to wait. I pray about a need for someone close to my heart and then run ahead of the Lord and try to fix it myself. I ask God for something I believe is His will then work to accomplish it before I get an answer. I get myself in trouble or become frustrated and exhausted because I fail to give the Lord a chance to act before I do. Not a good idea.

I need to learn to pray and keep praying with anticipation and thankfulness even when prayers are hard and the waiting harder. This is a lifelong learning process. I need to settle my heart on God and wait on His answers and His timing. If I have chosen to believe in God and His Word, and I have, I have chosen to trust Him. I just need to *act* on that belief to learn patience with God's timing and, in turn, patience with myself and others. I can keep moving forward but, unlike Rosie, be sensitive to His Word and guidance and be patiently obedient when His plan turns me in a different direction. If I choose to ignore Him, He won't let me fall headlong but He may let me come to the end of my rope before He reels me in.

Be still before the LORD and wait patiently for Him...
Psalm 37:7

 Prepare for Patience.

Learn to take a deep breath and count to ten—or 100—whatever it takes when you are tempted to come undone. You will need to practice.

Didn't I just talk about my adorable grandsons under "Slow Down?" Didn't I write about how patient I am with their "little boy ways?" Well, God must have gotten a laugh out of that because the very next day I was ready to put them both out on the curb with FREE signs taped to their shirts. Emitt didn't have school and picked on his little brother for entertainment. Garrison delivered ear-piercing screams when touched or looked at by Emitt. They both had runny noses and I couldn't figure out how to get their new TV to work. Garrison spilled his cereal on the floor. "Oh, oh," he chirped enthusiastically, making me wonder if it was an accident. Ranger, the dog, walked through the milk and tracked it around the kitchen.

Emitt started chanting, "I want breakfast from McDonald's," in his best whiny voice.

"No. Grandma made you a perfectly good breakfast now *eat it.*"

It was raining out so no bargaining chip of a trip to the park and Rich had to work so no back-up. They double-teamed me and I could feel myself begin to unravel. I glanced at the clock. It was 7:30 a.m. Only seven hours to go.

What does a good grandma do when she's losing it? She hides in the bathroom that's what she does. She prays hard for patience and when she can't stand the banging on the door any longer, loads everyone in the car and takes them to her house where she knows how to operate the TV.

I made several trips to the bathroom during the morning to mend my shredded nerves. Stepping out of the chaos for even a couple of minutes and asking God for HELP calmed me down and enabled me to open the door and rejoin my little darlings with a new perspective and even a touch of humor. By lunchtime we were all asleep on the

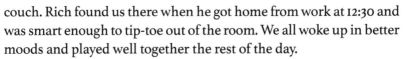

couch. Rich found us there when he got home from work at 12:30 and was smart enough to tip-toe out of the room. We all woke up in better moods and played well together the rest of the day.

What did I learn? Even though I'm a grown-up, it's very easy to lose control. My patience will be tested, often in unexpected ways. If I have a plan for dealing with surprise attacks, I stand a better chance of not acting on my feelings. Sometimes I need to distance myself from stressful people or situations even if it's only closing my eyes and counting to ten—or higher if I can swing it. I also learned not to take God or patience for granted.

> *Yet those who wait for the LORD will gain new strength;*
> *they will mount up with wings like eagles, they will run and not get tired,*
> *they will walk and not become weary.*
> Isaiah 40:31 NASB

Praying for patience is always risky but I trust God. When I pray and "wait for the LORD" I truly do gain new strength and patience for the day.

Look for the blessing in the inconveniences of life.

Webster defines inconvenient as, "not favorable to one's comfort, causing bother." These bothersome discomforts come in all shapes and sizes and can sorely test our patience. From a major life change to making a poor choice changing lines at the grocery store, our lives are filled with unplanned twists and turns. I suppose, as Christians, we shouldn't be surprised, but we usually are. God *does* warn us:

> *In his heart a man plans his course, but the Lord determines his steps.*
> Proverbs 16:9

I heard a friend say, "Life is what happens when you're planning something else." Is that ever the truth! However, I have found that long lines and detours frequently hold pleasant surprises and divine appointments if I'm patient and paying attention.

I'm not talking about tragedies or overwhelming circumstances although in God's perfect timing blessings may be revealed even there. I'm referring to the daily upsets or life changes that aren't written in our day planner or listed among our twelve-month goals (or the kitchen calendar on the fridge).

Where is the blessing in waiting patiently for over an hour on a cold exam table wrapped in a paper sheet? Hmmm, let's see. I had time to flip through several magazines which I don't often get to do. I found a great recipe in *Cuisine* and copied it onto the back of a receipt I retrieved from my purse (my mother would have torn it out). I was able to offer up a prayer for the poor man in the next room with a terrible cough, although I was a bit concerned about the germs blowing through the ventilation system. I thanked God I only needed a routine exam.

As a result of remaining patient and thinking about blessings in the middle of an inconvenience, I greeted the doctor with a smile when she finally arrived looking frazzled. "Take a deep breath," I said. She sat down and took a breath. "How long have you been waiting?" she asked. "Oh, about an hour but I've enjoyed your magazines and had a chance to examine all the blue veins in my legs." She laughed, apologized and began her exam.

I haven't always reacted this way. A simple statement by my mother many years ago caused me to look at the inconvenience of waiting and the blessing of patience from a different angle. We were Christmas shopping and the line we were in was long and slow. I groused about the wasted time and Mom said, "You know, honey, *everyone deserves their turn.* We can decide where to go for lunch while we wait." I never looked at long lines or delayed appointments the same way again. Everyone deserves their turn.

Sometimes you don't see the blessing right away. It was only after my Dad passed away that I realized how close Rich and I had become as we cared for Dad. I became aware that God gave me the chance to have a relationship with my father that was new to both of us. I learned to love my father with a softer, grown-up heart and view his life with clearer, grown-up eyes. With the passage of time I began to

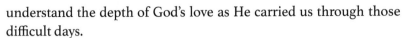

understand the depth of God's love as He carried us through those difficult days.

Uncovering a blessing is like looking for treasure but if we fail to patiently look we will surely fail to find. So keep your eyes open. We are surrounded by God's gifts every day, even in unlikely places. The longer I travel through this life the better I understand that God's hidden blessings and His lessons on patience are often the whole point of an inconvenience.

Do not boast about tomorrow, for you do not know
what a day may bring forth.
Proverbs 27:1

Patience

Sharing Fruit

 Lighten up when impatience strikes.

Not everything in life is a big deal requiring a big reaction yet sometimes I am so serious and impatient about the dumbest stuff. I have been known to come unglued and shoot my mouth off over trivial, non-life-threatening issues.

Let's take home improvement projects as an example. This comes quickly to mind as my husband is in the process of replacing the ancient deck in our back yard. Now, I have no idea how to build a deck so I immediately assume he doesn't either and proceed accordingly. I question all his plans and purchases and am not very subtle in letting him know I don't think he's capable of this undertaking. Before you know it we're barely talking and you can feel the tension in the house.

I should know to shut-up and trust him after forty-five years of successful free-lance plumbing, electrical, construction and myriad other assorted projects. Rich is very capable, knows how to read directions and, bless his heart, is willing to enter unfamiliar territory. He knows guy stuff—what can I say.

Well, unfortunately I say a lot and, instead of being supportive or at least staying away, I watch over his shoulder waiting for him to mess up. Lighten up, Annie! Take the man a glass of lemonade and say something nice like, "Honey, I really appreciate you hauling around those twenty-foot boards when it's ninety-five degrees out."

Actually, I should go do that now. He's hammering right outside the window. Be right back...

※ ※ ※

I'm back. He got a Diet Coke instead of lemonade but appreciated the gesture. I did not ask him why there was a twelve-inch gap at the ground that large animals could crawl under! The effort to hold it in exhausted me but I'm sure all will be well. I'm not positive, but pretty sure.

Of course there are heavy-duty things in life that require a serious response but very few events of daily living are helped by impatience and over-reacting. When I relax, go with the flow and refuse to take myself too seriously, life is much more pleasant and usually moves along just fine without me churning things up.

So, the next time I start to fret and get that old, familiar twinge of impatience with a person, a pet, my washing machine, or whatever life circumstance is annoying me at the moment, I need to stop before I act or open my mouth. I need to decide if the situation is worthy of an over-zealous or snide response. Would God prefer I take a deep breath and adopt an easy-going, patient attitude? Of course, I know the answer.

Therefore, as God's chosen people, holy and dearly loved, clothe yourselves with compassion, kindness, humility, gentleness and patience. Bear with each other and forgive whatever grievances you may have against one another. Forgive as the Lord forgave you.
Colossians 3:12-13

Patience requires flexibility.

I looked up the word flexible in my thesaurus. The word "stretchable" practically jumped off the page. The dictionary definitions, "able to bend without breaking" and "adjustable to change," also caught my attention. If I don't make a conscious effort to alter my mental attitude, I don't think these words will be said of me at my memorial service. Hopefully, I have time.

When I was a working woman (as opposed to whatever it is I am now) I was always the last one to get on board with a new procedure or change in policy, unless it was *my* idea. I would stubbornly hang on to what was familiar. What I knew how to do. I'm sure I exhausted my boss and fellow employees but they knew I needed time to process and patiently explained their plan and gave me time. I almost always got on board and then wondered why it took me so long to get there. I'm not flexible and don't adjust well to change, that's why.

Change in plans or spontaneous invitations make me nervous and I quickly become impatient and irritable with the person causing me such discomfort. Wouldn't it be easier all around if I had an open mind and a willingness to bend and stretch beyond my very limited comfort zone? Of course it would. I don't have to agree to everything, that could be dangerous, but I could loosen up and process ideas at a faster pace.

"How does Chinese food sound for dinner?" Rich asks hopefully.

"Oh, I don't know, let me think about it." I respond impatiently with my nose in a book.

Really? Do I have to cook? Do I get to spend time with my husband? What's to think about?

Why can't I just say, "Sounds great? What time do you want to go?"

Rich patiently waits while I wrap my brain around this complicated idea and then grabs the car keys before some unforeseen obstacle crosses my mind.

I may become impatient with other people but I'm beginning to realize how my lack of flexibility causes others to be impatient with *me*. Flexibility appears to be a two way street. I need to be bendable, open and agreeable toward others so I don't become impatient with them and they, in turn, don't become impatient with me. Wouldn't our relationships, jobs, and churches run with less friction and discord and more cooperation and harmony if we all learned to bend and adjust to each other, sort of like dancing? We may still step on each other's toes from time to time but we will, with practice, smile patiently and keep trying.

As a prisoner for the Lord, then, I urge you to live a life worthy of the calling you have received. Be completely humble and gentle; be patient, bearing with one another in love. Make every effort to keep the unity of the Spirit through the bond of peace.
Ephesians 4:1-3

 Hold your timetable loosely and begin to exercise patience.

Sometimes I find it hard to remember that other people aren't walking the same path or going the same direction I am. They may be traveling at a different speed. The world doesn't have to adjust to my schedule or pace. Impatience is the result of my forgetfulness.

Rich and I felt like we had been dropped into a strange parallel universe when my mother had a stroke. After ten days in the hospital she went into hospice care and we took her to our home. I've already talked about Rich, the almost-saint, but I have to mention him again. Mom fought taking her meds when she needed them which made me impatient and frustrated. I thought she was being stubborn when she was actually confused and probably trying to control the only thing left to her. Rich saw the situation differently and patiently soothed and comforted her during the difficult process. He endured sleeplessness, performed very challenging tasks and dealt with a grieving, slightly wacko wife without complaining or showing the least bit of resentment that his world had been turned upside down and his timetable put on hold.

Patience is inspired by mercy and mercy is tender-hearted, tolerant and compassionate. God knows I learn best through visual aids so he blessed me with a husband who demonstrated God's plan of mercy and patience toward my mother whose time was slowing to a stop.

It can be difficult to step off your path and onto someone else's. Take an elderly parent to the grocery store. You will need to be patient and sensitive to the frustration they feel, and may express, with the dependence and slowness that has overtaken their self-sufficiency. Play Play-Doh with a grandchild for two hours. Your patience is the key that grants you entry into a child's world. Drive a friend to her chemotherapy appointment and sit five hours in a room full of cancer patients. You will learn patience born of compassion in the face of such bravery. God gives us opportunities to show patience many times a day. From the trip to the grocery store in the morning to the meeting at church in the evening, patience is needed.

We like to think we are in control of our paths when, in reality, they go up and down hills, wind in curves and circles, take detours and endlessly cross, bump into or travel parallel to other people's paths. It's quite a journey. It demands open eyes and hearts and a willingness to set our agenda aside.

I will instruct you and teach you in the way you should go;
I will counsel you and watch over you.
Psalm 32:8

 Patiently give the benefit of the doubt (even when you're driving).

Freeway driving was a major part of my previous job. I am, by nature, a cautious, surface-street driver but I quickly developed freeway survival skills. I kept up with traffic, changed lanes only when absolutely necessary and never honked my horn unless my life was in danger.

Other drivers often seemed to look for a fight. They would weave in and out of traffic, honk at people who couldn't move even if they wanted to, make rude gestures and drive too fast. I did not make eye contact. These people scared me. I don't know what kind of day or life they experienced but it couldn't be good.

I hate to admit it, but I always felt a surge of righteous glee when I saw them farther down the road pulled over by a policeman. Yes! Justice is served.

My righteousness turned to humility one night as I watched the local news. A man was pulled over for speeding and honking on the same freeway I had been on two hours earlier. Instead of getting a ticket, he and the policeman delivered a baby girl in the backseat of the family van. The man had been frantically trying to get to the hospital on time. The news showed a grateful and very relieved couple holding their new daughter wrapped in Dad's jacket. The policeman was grinning from ear to ear.

God reminded me that evening that He is the only One who sees the big picture. We simply don't know what is going on in someone else's life to cause their behavior. Marriage problems, work stress, health issues, rebellious children, financial worries, new babies... the list is long. We don't need to condone bad or dangerous behavior but we can cut people some slack and show humility and patience when we don't understand their actions. After all, how many problems preoccupy our minds? How many mistakes have we made?

We may never know what causes people to be grouchy or rude, reckless or overbearing. And they don't know our reasons when we misbehave. So, the next time we take exception to someone's words or actions, let's take a deep breath of patience and breathe out the benefit of the doubt. There is always more to the story.

Love is patient...
1 Corinthians 13:4

🍇 **Be patient with yourself and you'll be more patient with others.**

How do we talk to ourselves when we're on a diet and the scales go up instead of down? What thoughts go through our mind when we have read the directions and still don't understand the new computer program or the cute little phone we got for our birthday? Maybe we don't remember names or get busy and forget the cookies in the oven and there's nothing for the bake sale. How patient are we with ourselves?

If you're like me, you're harder on yourself than you would be on anyone else.

"Why did you eat that peanut butter sandwich in the middle of the night? You're never going to lose weight. What a slob."

"I'm never going to get the hang of this new computer. Other people can figure it out. I'm just too dumb."

"Why am I forgetting things? I have so much to do I can't afford to be losing it already."

When I am impatient and angry with myself and my weaknesses, I am not usually a very nice person to be around. I'm grouchy with my family and withdraw from friends. I climb into my pity-party costume and expect other people to fix my problem and make things right. I'm snappy. I frown. No one would guess from my behavior that I'm a follower of Christ with a basket of fruit to deliver.

We often expect so much more of ourselves than God does. He loves us so much. We are His little girls and His patience with us knows no bounds. So let's step back and look at this child He loves and try to see her through His eyes and show her His patience.

"It's OK, you were hungry. You made good choices all day yesterday and only had a salad for dinner. Your body probably thought it was starving and needed that peanut butter sandwich. You're only up a pound. It's probably water weight from the salt. Keep trying, you're doing fine."

"Annie, you are not dumb. Sign up for the class they offer and you'll catch on in no time."

You get the idea. Talk to yourself like you would a friend or the little girl you once were. If you have a picture of yourself as a child, put it somewhere you'll see every day. Smile at her. Let go of impatience with yourself and listen for the voice of God rather than your inner-critic. You will be a much nicer person and your patience will extend to those around you.

Bless the LORD, O my soul; and all that is within me, bless His holy name.
Bless the LORD, O my soul, and forget none of His benefits;
Who pardons all your iniquities; Who heals all your diseases;
Who redeems your life from the pit;
Who crowns you with loving kindness and compassion;

Who satisfies your years with good things,
So that your youth is renewed like the eagle.
The LORD performs righteous deeds,
And judgments for all who are oppressed.
He made known His ways to Moses, His acts to the sons of Israel.
The LORD is compassionate and gracious,
Slow to anger and abounding in lovingkindness,
He will not always strive with us; Nor will He keep His anger forever.
He has not dealt with us according to our sins,
Nor rewarded us according to our iniquities.
For as high as the heavens are above the earth
So great is His lovingkindness toward those who fear Him.
As far as the east is from the west,
So far has He removed our transgressions from us.
Just as a father has compassion on his children,
So the LORD has compassion on those who fear Him.
For He Himself knows our frame; He is mindful that we are but dust.
Psalm 103:1-14 NASB

If God shows such love and patience toward our dusty selves, who are we to argue? Accept His gift and share it with the world around you.

FRUIT FOR THOUGHT

Patience

Nurturing Fruit

1. Is slowing down and being patient a challenge for you? Do you tend to be controlled by your "to do" list? What areas of your life need your patient attention?

2. What or who challenges your patience? Do you let your negative feelings spill over into other people's lives? Sigh! Do you know anyone (including you) who plays the victim? How could you be more positive in your response or behavior?

3. Do you identify with Rosie? Why or why not? Have you ever ignored God and suffered the consequences of impatience?

4. When your patience is tested (and it will be) how do you respond? In what areas do you need to practice preparing for patience?

5. Do you respond with patience to inconveniences or unplanned circumstances? Have you ever found unexpected treasure when life doesn't go as you planned? Are you looking?

Sharing Fruit

1. Are there areas of your life where you could lighten up when impatience strikes?

2. What are your thoughts about patience requiring flexibility? Are you able to be open-minded and willing to step out of your comfort zone to obey God's will? Is it a huge step or are you already there? Give examples of how you respond to different situations.

3. Have you experienced stepping off your path and onto some else's? What did you learn about patience? What does your willingness to enter into someone else's situation say to the people involved?

4. Do you stand your ground at all cost or are you able to patiently grant the benefit of the doubt to others? Are there times others have patiently granted you grace when you goofed?

5. Listen to your self-talk. Are you less patient with yourself than God or others would be? How does a negative attitude and impatience toward yourself impact others? Name one area where this is a struggle.

❄ ❄ ❄

Grab your notebook and write out...

❖ One Scripture from this chapter that is particularly meaningful to you.

❖ Your Thoughts and Stories

❄ ❄ ❄

Chapter Five

THE FRUIT OF THE SPIRIT IS ... KINDNESS

Eddie from Manchester

"Excuse me, miss."

I turned around as I dropped the third can of pork and beans into my cart. Next to me, blocking the aisle stood an elderly man, an Englishman by his thick accent.

"I know you don't work here but are those beans on sale? They're not on the missus' list but if they're cheap maybe I should get some."

He wore the traditional "old man" uniform—khaki slacks, a plaid shirt and light-weight beige jacket. My dad and father-in-law had both worn the same familiar clothing. I smiled. I like a man in uniform and love accents of any kind. I was immediately drawn into "grocery store" conversation.

"Yes. They're three cans for a dollar which is good if you like pork and beans."

"They're not on the list, though." He read the piece of paper in his hand as if he might have missed *beans*. "I'd better not. The missus suffered a bit of a stroke and I don't want to upset her."

"I'm sorry. That has to be hard for both of you," I said, feeling a prickle behind my eyes.

"It is," he paused, "and I had to have my Jake put down yesterday."

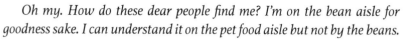

Oh my. How do these dear people find me? I'm on the bean aisle for goodness sake. I can understand it on the pet food aisle but not by the beans.

"Oh dear. Was Jake your dog?"

"That he was. A purebred. I can't think of the breed. It's from Japan."

I searched through my limited dog knowledge and the word Akita popped out.

"Yes, that's it, an Akita. A big old boy, 80 pounds he was. Fourteen years old and healthy as can be until few months ago. He started coughing and losing weight. The vet said it was his heart. Nothing they could do."

"I'm so sorry. It's hard to lose such a long-time friend."

"An old friend he was, miss." His hand reached up and touched his heart.

I glanced behind us at the people piling up down the aisle.

"Let's move over here, so these people can get to the beans," I said. We pushed our carts to an out of the way space in front of a battery display.

"His registered name was…" He rattled off a long Japanese name with a Jake sound somewhere in the middle. "So we just called him Jake."

"A good name," I said.

"He was my dog. He loved the missus too but he never left my side. He took part of my heart with him when he passed."

Lord, I'm going to lose it right here in the store. Help me be what this man needs me to be right now.

"It's a gift to have a friend like that," I said. "A gift to you and to Jake."

"Yes, but it's hard when you outlive such a gift." Hand to the heart again. "I had an Irish Wolfhound before Jake, name of Tommy. Raised him from a pup and he was a fine one. Had him when we lived in Chicago and it broke my heart when he passed. I can tell you this for sure, though, miss. When I go, Jake and Tommy will be with me. Whether I go up or down they'll be at my side."

I nodded. Not much of a comeback to that. Finally, in an attempt to get off the dead dog subject, I said, "From your accent it sounds like you're from England, am I right?"

"Yes, miss, I'm from Manchester. That was home until the missus and I moved here after the war. We raised our two boys in Chicago

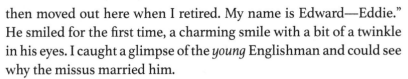

then moved out here when I retired. My name is Edward—Eddie." He smiled for the first time, a charming smile with a bit of a twinkle in his eyes. I caught a glimpse of the *young* Englishman and could see why the missus married him.

"My name is Annie. Nice to meet you, Eddie"

"No one talks much anymore," he said, his smile fading. "My boys are busy working or on their computers. The grandchildren, bless 'em, have their own lives. My neighbors keep changing and I barely know them. Back in Manchester we knew everyone in the neighborhood. Couldn't walk down the street without stopping two or three times for a chat. People helped each other when there were troubles. You felt a belonging," he stopped and looked around.

"Raising our boys we were part of the community," he continued, "kids coming and going. I had my work and the missus was busy caring for all of us. The years in Chicago were good ones. We like it here but as we've gotten older it's as if no one sees us anymore." He didn't seem to be feeling sorry for himself, just stating a fact.

"What brought you to Portland?" I asked.

"The boys took jobs out here and my brother, rest his soul, lived in Portland. We bought a house on the bluff in Sellwood and been here now over twenty years."

"I grew up just a few blocks from where you live," I said. "My parents bought a house in Westmoreland right after the war. They lived there until my dad died a few years ago."

"Well, it's a small world now, isn't it miss?" He glanced at the check-out lines. "I've enjoyed talking to you and do appreciate your caring about my Jake."

"It's been good talking to you too Eddie."

"I'd best be on my way. The missus will be wondering where I am. The lines are short, we'd better get in one."

"I'm not quite done shopping," I said. "I still have to buy a birthday card." I began to turn my cart the other way.

"It's good-bye then. You take care, miss."

"You take care too, Eddie. Have a good day."

The tears welled up as I walked away.

Yes, you take care Eddie from Manchester. You were a gift to me and a reminder of how much we need to see and hear each other. I'll be praying for you and the missus and keeping an eye out for you on the bean aisle.

$\mathscr{K}$*indness*

Nurturing Fruit

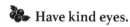 **Have kind eyes.**

Let's ask God to give us eyes that see one person at a time. Eyes that see and acknowledge another person's existence. There are no invisible people to God. The people He puts in our path need to know we see them. The rumpled man on the freeway exit with the cardboard sign we pretend not to notice. The handicapped person at church who makes us uncomfortable so we look away. The young mother with three crying children in the store we choose to ignore. And Eddie from Manchester. They are all visible to God.

What would He do? He would put *us* there in that time and place to see, to smile, to help. He calls us to be His eyes. You can't fix everything, give money to everyone or change every circumstance that comes your way but you can see and acknowledge that you know and you care. Do and give what you can but make sure you see with eyes that reflect the light and kindness of our God.

I once worked for a women's ministry. At the end of each session the client was asked to fill out an evaluation form about our services and her counselor. I would read through these forms at the end of the day to see if anything stood out, good or bad. There was a question at the end regarding the client's feelings about her counselor and I almost always read good reports.

One rainy afternoon became particularly hectic. There were several walk-in clients as well as those with appointments. Damp coats and drippy umbrellas raised the humidity level to sticky. Small children and toddlers with questionable diapers ran through the waiting room. The phone rang non-stop. All the counseling rooms were full and clients overflowed into my office.

We were all exhausted at the end of the day. I sat at my desk checking files when I leaned back in my chair and smiled as God reminded me why we were all there. One of the counselor evaluations simply said, "She had kind eyes. Thank you."

In the middle of a chaotic day, the counselor shut out the noise and confusion and focused on the woman in front of her. She filled out all the required paper-work. I'm sure she helped the woman work through her situation and gave her good referrals and resources. The client came away with helpful information and personal encouragement but that's not what she chose to write down. She remembered kind eyes. I knew she saw Jesus' eyes. I've never forgotten.

You are the light of the world. A city on a hill cannot be hidden.
Neither do people light a lamp and put it under a bowl. Instead they put
it on its stand, and it gives light to everyone in the house. In the same
way, let your light shine before men, that they may see your good
deeds and praise your Father in heaven.
Matthew 15:14-16

🌼 Settle down and acknowledge God's kindness to you.

I misjudged the time it would take to navigate three freeways and a bridge during morning rush-hour. Part of my job was to cover centers who were short-handed and I received an early morning call for help—a director in bed with the flu. I arrived at the office out of breath and slightly frazzled. I missed prayer time with the rest of the staff and volunteers.

Connie, the receptionist, a young woman I hadn't met, asked if I would like her to pray with me.

"Yes, thank you. That would be wonderful. Hang on while I grab a cup of coffee."

We went into the ailing Director's office and chatted for a few minutes to get to know each other and then discussed the prayer needs of the center. Connie appeared calm and quiet compared to my now caffeinated self. We lifted the needs of the center and staff to the Lord and then Connie said, "Lord, please settle Annie's heart. Bathe her in Your compassion and kindness as she moves into this day doing Your work."

I know she said more but I was stuck on her request to settle my heart. Of course she was aware I was a bit unraveled upon arrival but she had no way of knowing she lifted a *chronically* unsettled heart before the Lord.

I gradually felt peace wash over me. Connie's prayer for me to experience God's kindness opened a window so I could see that my kindness diminished in direct proportion to an increase in my anxiety and frustration. My heart had been agitated and distracted for far too long and it was starting to show. I needed to rest in God's arms and let Him calm me. I needed to accept His kindness and trust Him. Only then could my heart be at peace and His kindness flow through me.

I think Connie was a bit surprised as I hugged and thanked her. God used her prayer to begin the process of directing my busy and anxious heart toward "the peace of God that surpasses all comprehension..." (Philippians 4:7 NASB).

Does this story resonate with you? Perhaps a window just opened and you caught a glimpse of your own overwrought heart. If so, I pray right now that God pulls you onto His lap, and settles your heart as he bathes you in His kindness and peace.

*Don't fret or worry. Instead of worrying, pray. Let petitions
and praises shape your worries into prayers, letting God know your
concerns. Before you know it, a sense of God's wholeness, everything
coming together for good, will come and settle you down.
It's wonderful what happens when Christ displaces worry
at the center of your life.*
Philippians 4:6-7 MSG

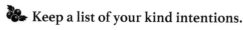 **Keep a list of your kind intentions.**

If I got credit for my kind intentions I would be a saint. Unfortunately, most of the ideas that pop into my head regarding acts of kindness toward others never pop into reality. I forget to check the calendar for birthdays so usually send belated birthday cards. I procrastinate when it comes to visiting someone in the hospital and when they go home I put off calling and taking a meal until too much time has gone by. I could make a long list of good, creative, helpful ideas that never got off the ground but I think I'll wait until tomorrow.

Back in my procrastinating employee days I developed a simple-stupid system that works for me as long as I do it (there's always a catch). It started with a quote I read on a classroom wall at a writing seminar. "Listen to the voice in your head and leave tracks of your thinking." I suppose it's a glorified to-do list but I try not to think of it that way.

First, purchase a steno pad and write down creative ideas, current birthdays, out-of-the-ordinary daily tasks, phone calls to make, e-mails to check and respond to, notes to send, gifts to buy, everything you currently want and/or need to remember or accomplish. A no-brainer, right? If you're technologically inclined, and you probably are, I'm sure there's an app for your iPad, computer or phone that would work for you. I'm sticking with the cheap steno pad.

You can use numbers or bullet points, it doesn't matter. Then check off or draw a line through each completed item. It's very satisfying. The rule is you can't flip the page until everything is done on the current page. Then you draw a line across the page or a giant red "X," whatever makes you happy, and move on to the next page. Now, realistically, you are frequently going to run out of room on a page before you have completed everything. So, transfer the not yet completed items from the first page to the second and go ahead and scratch off the previous page. Re-writing the things you haven't done is a great reminder/guilt inducer so, hopefully, you won't have things that carry over throughout the entire notebook. Sometimes I decide something is a dumb idea and let it go but, usually, things get done. I also put projects on a separate page as they tend to bog down the process.

One more thing, then I'll leave you alone to get started (if you have this problem). I have things that come to mind I call "God prompts." These are ideas and actions that I know came from God because they didn't come from me. If the Holy Spirit is nudging (or poking) me to get my attention and activate a specific action, I need to hop to it. I put a star by these and try not to carry them forward. Sometimes there's no time to write it down. I need to act promptly before the appropriate moment slips away. I can write it down and check it off later.

This simple technique is fun because it combines things I really like:

* I love to make lists and check things off. It's fun to see what I've accomplished.
* My brain is free to be open and creative since it isn't bogged down trying to remember all that needs doing. I don't have to remember to remember.
* I don't feel guilty or burdened all the time.
* I enjoy prayerfully considering the "God prompts" and asking for the Holy Spirit's help to respond in a way that demonstrates kindness to those in my world.

If this sounds like something that would be helpful for you, have fun with it. Ask God what He wants on your list and start writing. You will be blessed and you will bless others as order is created, mental freedom is restored and the job gets done. If your mind and heart are open to "God prompts," He will show you where a bit of kindness is needed.

Note: This works for me but if it sounds like a pain in the neck to you, or one more thing to do, skip it. God will free your heart for kindness in a way that works for you.

Remember, too, that knowing what is right to do and
then not doing it is sin.
James 4:17 TLB

Practice being kind to yourself.

Treat yourself the way you would like to be treated.

In Leviticus 19:18 we are commanded to "...love your neighbor as yourself..." God is saying we are to love ourselves so we are able to love our neighbors. I believe our unkindness and lack of love toward others often stems from anger or disappointment with ourselves. We simply don't love ourselves very much. Some days I can't even work up a "like."

I've gone through several stretches in my adult life, as a Christian, where I've been withdrawn, cold and sometimes downright nasty to the people I live with. I put on a cheerful, nice-lady mask when I walk out the door because I want to be liked, but on goes the mean-lady mask when I come home. Yes, they're both masks because neither one reflect the heart attitude God wants me to have.

Why is this? I think it's because I'm often not happy with myself. I have allowed some habit or grudge or bitterness or the frustration of unrealistic, unattainable expectations or some other crummy thing (a.k.a. fruit fly), gain a foothold in my life. Part of me wants to break the bondage and part of me doesn't want to let go. Result? Major inner conflict, grouchiness toward those closest to me and a distancing in relationships, including God.

Now, I think if I had a friend I knew was struggling, I would come alongside with love and support.

Can I do the same for myself? Will I let go of my pride and ask those closest to me for help? Can I trust God's Word?

Well, I choose to answer a resounding, heartfelt and slightly desperate, "YES." I decided to treat myself with understanding, respect, forgiveness and genuine kindness. *I know* God is faithful and will see me through.

I will always have flaws and weaknesses but I will acknowledge my humanity and accept God's unconditional love and grace. I will ask for help when needed, lean on the Lord and give myself a kindly, encouraging pat on the back.

When I see myself as someone worthy of love, because I am totally loved by God, and treat myself with kindness, the masks begin to crumble and the "me" that emerges will become the real-deal God created. A woman who experiences kindness turned inward can now let God help her begin to turn kindness outward.

So do not fear, for I am with you; do not be dismayed, for I am your God.
I will strengthen you and help you; I will uphold you with
my righteous right hand.
Isaiah 41:10

 Ask God for wisdom and discernment to activate kindness.

As a new believer I was in a prayer group with Barbara, a woman who prayed for wisdom and discernment when she was facing difficult situations. Being fairly new to the game, I asked her why she often asked God for those particular attributes.

"Well, Annie, in my job I often feel overwhelmed with the needs of others. I need help. I pray for wisdom and discernment to understand what is really needed and to know what God wants me to do in each particular situation. I also have two teenage daughters." She smiled and rolled her eyes.

Later, I headed for the dictionary. I knew the Bible stressed wisdom and discernment but I needed Webster's definitions to help me out.

"Wisdom" was defined as good judgment, informed, prudent, reasoning, clear thinking, understanding, practical knowledge, carefulness, tact, balance, stability and common sense. "Discernment" meant to perceive or recognize clearly, be discriminating and perceptive. Webster then sent me off to the word "discreet" which means being careful about what one says or does, vigilant, sensible, circumspect and attentive.

Now I possessed a better understanding of the words themselves, I thought it would be a good idea to see what God says on the subject. I went to my Strong's concordance and was a bit overwhelmed. Apparently wisdom is very important to God as there are, by my count, 232 verses on the subject. Wow. If sheer volume is the measuring stick, wisdom is a biggie. I needed to pare down a bit so went to the mini-concordance in the back of my Bible. I looked up lots of verses but this one helped me realize I needed to be praying for wisdom for myself.

But if any of you lacks wisdom, let him ask of God, who gives to all men
generously and without reproach, and it will be given to him.
James 1:5 NASB

The following verse made spiritual discernment clearer to me.

For everyone who partakes only of milk is not accustomed to the word
of righteousness, for he is a babe. But solid food is for the mature, who
because of practice have their senses trained to discern good and evil.
Hebrews 5:13-14 NASB

The note in my New American Standard Bible on this verse says, "The truly wise seek and commonly find the proper time for every action." Very helpful. Wisdom and discernment are needed to demonstrate every Fruit of the Spirit. I chose to focus on prayer for wisdom and discernment in cultivating kindness because it requires wisdom to have spiritual understanding and walk in a manner worthy of God's will. It takes discernment to perceive specifically what action is needed.

...a wise man's heart discerns both time and judgment.
Ecclesiastes 8:5 NKJV

Kindness

Sharing Fruit

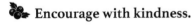 **Encourage with kindness.**

"You are the slowest checker I've ever seen. Who taught you how to bag groceries? No one, I can tell!" The lady (I use the term loosely) at the head of the line berated the young man as he tried to keep a pleasant look on his face.

"I'm sorry you're unhappy, ma'am. Can I call someone to carry your bags to the car?"

"No. I suppose I look like an old lady to you?" she snapped back. He wisely kept his mouth shut.

At this point, the man behind her chimed in, "Would you two quit yakking. I haven't got all day." The checker looked shell-shocked.

The store was busy and I was fourth in line. Fortunately, the lady ahead of me was no wimp.

"Leave the boy alone, he's doing a fine job," she said evenly but loud enough so the two in front of her could hear. Fortunately, they ignored her and moved on. The poor boy was probably envisioning a brawl at his check-out.

"You do excellent work," she said when it was her turn. "I don't know what gets into some people to be so unkind."

"Thank you," he said rather shakily. "It takes a lot of nice customers to help me recuperate from the grouchy ones."

At this point I had to join in. "Let me be the next customer who thinks you are doing great," I said with a big smile. There was no one behind me so we chatted briefly until I got a smile in return.

I left the store hoping the poor kid wouldn't suffer from post-traumatic stress disorder. I've worked with the public and it isn't always easy.

I've read it takes up to ten positive comments to counteract one negative. Out of the blue, the words to *Home on the Range* popped into my head:

"Oh give me a home where the buffalo roam and the deer
and the antelope play.
Where seldom is heard a discouraging word and the skies
are not cloudy all day."

We can't control everyone else, but wouldn't it be nice if we chose words of encouragement to give to others. Words that build up instead of tear down. I am ashamed of myself when I think how often I don't control my mouth and shoot negative words into the hearts of those I love the most.

I don't know about the buffalo and antelope roaming around and we need a little rain but I sure like the sound of a world where discouraging words are seldom heard.

> *But encourage one another daily, as long as it is called Today,*
> *so that none of you may be hardened by sin's deceitfulness.*
> Hebrews 3:13

> *Therefore encourage one another and build each other up...*
> 1 Thessalonians 5:11

🐝 Watch your "buts," and avoid being a "sneaky sniper" or "jokester." They can squash kindness.

"Buts"

I recently overheard this comment while waiting for a seat in a restaurant. I didn't even have to eavesdrop, these women were sitting right next to me.

"Connie, you look lovely in that color blue but that style of dress really isn't very flattering on you."

All Connie could come back with was, "Oh." You can't really say, "Thank you" to a statement like that. I'm sure the comment on the unflattering style of her dress is all she heard. It probably ruined her lunch. I picked up the offense on her behalf and am dealing with it here.

Don't do that! Anytime a critical "but" follows a comment or compliment, the only thing heard is what comes after the "but." Usually criticism. I think this is often a deliberate mixed message. What we really want to say is the negative comment and somehow think if we precede it with something nice it will soften the blow. It doesn't. It can be hurtful and confusing and leaves the person on the receiving end without much of a comeback.

I don't know about you but I do this unconsciously all the time and don't even think a thing about it unless it's done to me.

I've become more sensitive to this issue since the "blue dress" incident. I want you to know how happy I am that you're still reading. No, "buts" about it.

> *...from the same mouth come both blessing and cursing.*
> *My brethren, these things ought not to be this way.*
> *Does a fountain send out from the same opening both*
> *fresh and bitter water?*
> James 3:10-11 NASB

"Sneaky Snipers"

Anytime you start a sentence with, "I don't want to hurt your feelings ..." the person's feelings will inevitably be hurt. Same with, "Don't take this wrong..." It guarantees whatever follows will be taken wrong, probably accompanied by anger or a wounded heart.

The principle is the same as with "buts." We really want to say something derogatory but try to weasel out of responsibility by telling the poor soul we don't want to hurt them. I call these comments, "sneaky snipers" because you don't usually see them coming and they aim to inflict pain.

"Annie, I don't want to hurt your feelings, however, you've really packed on some weight since Christmas." *Really? Like I hadn't noticed?*

> *A fool finds no pleasure in understanding but delights*
> *in airing his own opinions.*
> Proverbs 18:2

"Jokesters"

Another more obvious type of kindness killer is the jokester. This person comes right out and says whatever crummy thing she wants and, if you dare take exception to it, says, "I was only kidding. Can't you take a joke?" *No, I guess I can't.*

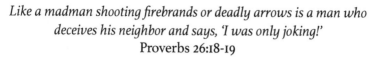
*Like a madman shooting firebrands or deadly arrows is a man who
deceives his neighbor and says, 'I was only joking!'*
Proverbs 26:18-19

Simple kindness.

The people close to you, acquaintances and those you bump into
during the course of your day need to be treated tenderly and thought-
fully. Most of us try not to look needy, but we are. From the moment we
enter this world until the day we exit we crave simple human kindness.

We all have memories of being treated unkindly. Those memories
tend to stick like gum on your shoe. Acts of kindness, however, sparkle in our memories and leave us feeling loved. That's what kindness
is all about: love for others inspired by God's love for us.

One year in elementary school I had a split class. We had a man in
the morning and a woman in the afternoon. I was shy and didn't raise
my hand much in class and the morning teacher chose to constantly
ridicule and make unkind remarks about me and another girl. He
would encourage the other students to laugh at us. My mornings
were a nightmare and I still get a quick rush of fear when I think of
him even though, from my adult perspective, I know he must have
experienced difficult things in his own life to behave the way he did.

The afternoons were a completely different experience. The
young woman who taught the class was kind, compassionate and
nurturing. I think she knew what my mornings were like as she often
kept me by her side helping with simple tasks. I flourished under her
kindness. I talked and raised my hand, developed my creativity and
joined in the activities with the rest of the class.

When my mother went to conferences she said it felt like she had
two completely different children. She did. One shy, humiliated and
withdrawn. One talkative, confident and outgoing.

Looking back, those are some of the most vivid memories I have
of grade school.

The darkness of cruelty and unkindness versus the warm, bright
light of a kind and loving heart. It was a hard year but I think it was
worth it.

I believe we are called to be kind, warm-hearted and compassionate. We are responsible for our actions regardless of how we feel or the response we get from others, (although even a "hard nut" will sometimes crack when shown friendliness and understanding). Kindness is our love for God demonstrated to the world around us.

It's an especially tasty piece of fruit.

She opens her mouth in wisdom, and the teaching of kindness
is on her tongue.
Proverbs 31:26 NASB

Kindness acknowledges other people exist.

Have you ever been in a situation where you felt invisible? At a party? A meeting? An office waiting room? Whatever the circumstance, you feel awkward, uncomfortable and embarrassed. You're not sure what to do. If you're an extrovert, you might speak right up and make your presence known. If you're an introvert, you can sit down and wait to be noticed or leave. You should never have to do either. You are not invisible!

I realize you can't control how other people treat you but you can make sure it's not how you treat others. Jesus *saw* people, even the *invisible* ones other people overlooked. Here are a few tips to help us "see" other people.

- If someone appears to be at loose ends at a party or gathering, go talk to them. Introduce yourself and then introduce them to others, even if it's out of your comfort zone. Always use people's names if at all possible. If you're the hostess, you might ask the uncomfortable newcomer if they would mind helping you. A job always helps.
- If you're in charge of a Bible study or a meeting people gave their valuable time to attend, introduce everyone (nametags are good) and emphasize that you value *everyone's* participation and input. You have to act fast before the "type A's" or perpetually needy people take over and everyone else fades into

the background and starts mentally checking out or looking for their coats. A bit of unrelated advice: start on time.

- If you work in a front desk position or any job where you meet the public, make eye contact, smile and acknowledge whoever comes through the door. From a crowded doctor's office to a restaurant on a Friday night, people are much more willing to wait if they know they have been "seen."
- Smile when you answer the phone, it can be heard on the other end.
- Don't pretend you can't see the elderly, the handicapped or the homeless. Sometimes looking a person in the eye, smiling and saying, "Hello," is all it takes to cause them to feel noticed as a real person. I mentioned this under "Have Kind Eyes" but I think it's important enough to bring up again.

Whatever the situation, you can't go wrong with a genuine smile as you look a person in the eye and say, "Hi."

And He saw a certain poor widow putting in two small copper coins.
Luke 21:1-2 NASB

But Jesus turning and seeing her said, "Daughter take courage; your faith has made you well."
Matthew 9:22 NASB

Give clear directions. Kindness shows the way.

I don't know about you but when I'm in an uncomfortable or unfamiliar situation I tend to feel out of control and nervous. Recently, on my first visit to a new doctor's office, it wasn't made clear what to do with my paperwork when I was done. I went to the receptionist and was told to give it to the nurse when she called me. This was no big deal but she could have mentioned it when she gave me the clipboard. Everything else went well until I came out of the exam room. I had no idea which way to go.

Coming in I blindly followed the nurse, preoccupied about getting on the scales. Now, without a guide, I faced the maze of hallways feeling abandoned and not too bright. I'm sure there was an exit sign but I must have missed it as I ended up behind the reception desk. I eventually found my way out but I'm sure my blood pressure was much higher than when I went in.

I probably would have thought it was just me and my poor sense of direction until I went to a local hospital for my mammogram. What a difference! The technician came to the waiting room, called my name and introduced herself. Every step of the way she kindly explained exactly what I was to do and what she was going to do. I knew how to put on the gown, where to put my clothes and purse and what to do with the key to the locker. When gowned up I simply stepped out of the room where she stood waiting for me.

She made every step of the procedure clear and answered as many of my questions as she could. We also chatted and laughed—during a mammogram! Needless to say, I wasn't feeling stressed. When we were done, she walked me back to the dressing room, waited outside until I was ready and walked me back to the lobby. I thanked her and told her she should teach seminars on how kindness and respect de-stress patients.

Years later, I worked with women facing stressful life situations. Making an appointment and walking through the front door was often difficult for them and we did what we could to calm their nerves. The women were greeted with a kind expression from the receptionist when they came through the front door and the paperwork clearly explained. Their peer-counselor would greet them in the waiting room, introduce herself and, when they were in the counseling room, kindly explain step-by-step what was going to happen. The better we explained things the more the client relaxed and felt in control. We called this giving the client a "road map" so she would know where she was going and what to expect. At the end of the visit we would walk her to the door as we would a guest leaving our home.

Regardless of the situation, if we keep our antenna up, the Holy Spirit will show us how to step into the lives of those we encounter who may be in a difficult, confusing, or embarrassing situation. He will help us to kindly do what we can to calm, clarify and ease awkward moments.

So when the lady next to you in the condiment aisle drops a jar of mayonnaise and is standing there frozen and looking mortified, come to her rescue. Tell her to stay put and you will tell the nearest employee there is a bit of mayo cleanup on aisle four. Take the paper towels out of your cart and help her clean her shoes while you tell her about the time you dropped a bottle of olive oil and slipped in it. Put a new jar of mayo in her basket and offer to help her with whatever else she may need once the clean-up crew arrives.

When someone is in distress they often can't see ahead to the next step. God may have given you the map to help them find their way. Even if there isn't a clear solution, your presence, kindness and willingness to step in and help can reduce stress, provide comfort and reassurance and give someone a glimpse of God. Jesus would have helped that lady with the mayonnaise in a heartbeat.

> *Then I heard the voice of the Lord, saying, "Whom shall I send,*
> *and who will go for Us?"*
> *Then I said, "Here am I. Send me!"*
> Isaiah 6:8 NASB

FRUIT FOR THOUGHT

Kindness

Nurturing Fruit

1. Have you experienced "kind eyes?" What thoughts come to mind from this phrase?

2. Do you often feel unsettled (not just from caffeine), anxious or frustrated? If yes, how does this lack of inner

peace effect your kindness toward others? Look up and pray Philippians 4:6-7 and ask God for a settled heart.

3. What do you think about keeping a list of kind intentions and actually following through? Is this something you struggle with?

4. Do you see the importance, despite your flaws and weaknesses, of loving and being kind to yourself? How does your attitude toward yourself influence others?

5. Why is wisdom and discernment needed to live out every Fruit of the Spirit—not just kindness? If you struggle in these areas, ask God for help.

...who gives to all men generously and without reproach...
James 1:5 NASB

Sharing Fruit

1. Have you ever been hurt by unkind or discouraging words? How did you feel? Did the experience give you more empathy toward others? List three ways you can encourage others this week.

2. Did the sections on "buts," "sneaky snipers" and "jokesters" sound familiar? If so, give an example. If you are the guilty party, ask God to help you hear these words and phrases and recognize the unkind attitude behind them before they pop out your mouth.

3. Do you have memories of being treated unkindly? How about memories of being treated with simple, genuine kindness? What can you learn about how to treat others from these experiences?

4. Have you ever felt invisible? What were the circumstances and how did you react? What can you do to *see* people in your sphere of influence?

5. Have you ever found yourself in an awkward situation where kind, clear directions or assistance would have been helpful? How could you be more aware and actively show kindness in awkward moments?

※ ※ ※

Grab your notebook and write out...

◆ One Scripture from this chapter that is particularly meaningful to you.

◆ Your Thoughts and Stories

※ ※ ※

Chapter Six

THE FRUIT OF THE SPIRIT IS ... GOODNESS

Mom

"Excuse me," my mother said to the woman in front of her on the escalator at Macy's. "What perfume do you have on? You smell delicious."

The woman turned around—a precarious move—and said "Thank you. It's Estee Lauder's *White Linen*. They carry it here and at Nordstrom's."

I had to move them along when we reached the bottom to avoid a pile-up of Christmas shoppers. They were discussing the benefits of "layering" scent with lotion and powder. Mom wrote the name of the cologne in the ever-present notebook she kept in her purse for just such occasions. The women said "good-bye" and both walked away smiling. Then the hunt was on for the *White Linen*.

We had to stop twice on our way to the perfume counter for Mom to talk to babies in strollers. "Aren't you the cutest little thing? What a beautiful smile." She didn't usually talk to the parents—just the babies—but the new moms and dads were obviously pleased.

This sort of thing happened everywhere we went. When Mom saw something she genuinely liked or was curious about she would comment on it to the person involved.

"Where do you get your hair done? I love the cut." Out would come the notebook.

"Thank you for the excellent service, you made our lunch even nicer. You must enjoy your work." (She was a good tipper too!)

As a child, she was a constant embarrassment to me but as I grew up I came to appreciate and enjoy her gift for sprinkling goodness into other's lives. She was never gushy and was careful not to take up other people's time. She just asked her question or made a comment and went about her business.

One day she called me and told me all the details about her friend Louise's new house. It sounded wonderful and I never heard a hint of, "Oh, I wish I had a house like that." Mom was always pleased for the success of others (especially me—her one-and-only) and never hesitated to say so and give her reasons.

Now Mom wasn't always sweetness and light. She could flip from feisty to melancholy and wasn't above a snide comment here and there. Her language could be a bit colorful and she dealt with the difficulties in her life with passive/aggressive brilliance. She possessed good qualities and faults but, Betty May, my dear mother, was the real deal.

She listened and heard and cared about what you said. She kept her eyes and ears open for opportunities to compliment someone and make their day. She never flattered, if she said it she meant it.

Mom was also generous with her time and money. When my boys were small she was always up for a trip to the park or zoo or mall. These outings usually included lunch which could be harrowing experiences with the kids. Mom always laughed instead of coming undone as I did (of course she was the Grandma so everything the boys did was adorable). She knew I needed her help and was truly a good sport. She knew her limits, though, and would never babysit both boys at the same time. Smart lady.

One year we didn't have enough money to pay the property taxes. I didn't know what to do and was desperately praying for help. I never said a word to my mother but a week before the taxes were due I received a card with a check for $1,000 inside. On the front of the card was a picture of a little girl sitting in a field blowing a dandelion "wish." Inside Mom wrote, "Dad and I thought this might come in handy. We love you more than you know."

I sat and sobbed.

As my mother grew older she began to slip away into the abyss of Alzheimer's. She was terrified by the awareness of what was happening to her. We still tried to get out at least once a week and traipse around to familiar places but she would panic if she lost sight of me. We went out to lunch a week before she suffered the stroke that took her life. She couldn't figure out how to unroll the silverware from the napkin so I reached across the table to help.

"Mom, you have the most beautiful hands," I said.

She looked up at me and the lost look disappeared for a moment. "Thank you. You're a good girl, do you know that?"

"Well, Mom, if I am, it's from hanging out with you all these years." She held tight to my hand and smiled.

※ ※ ※

I loved my mother and miss her very much. We had our ups and downs but my heart will always be entwined with hers. I have to laugh every time I stop to talk to babies or take the notebook out of my purse to jot down the name of someone's perfume.

Thank you, Lord, for giving me a mother who taught me how to be real. Help me keep my eyes open for the times when a little goodness is needed.

Goodness

Nurturing Fruit

 Remember, our goodness comes from God.

Kindness is our inward love of God resulting in a loving heart attitude toward others. *Goodness* is the action and work generated by the heart attitude of kindness.

As Christians, we may do all sorts of good things for others. However, if we are not in fellowship with God we may be seeking our own glory not His.

There are many non-believers who work selflessly for the benefit of others because they genuinely care. There are others who serve out of selfish motives. Either way, good things are accomplished but God does not get the credit.

If we say we follow Christ yet serve strictly within the boundaries of our comfort zones or for personal recognition and praise, we might want to examine our motives. There's nothing wrong in receiving compliments and encouragement for what we're doing, it feels good and keeps us going. However, we need to prayerfully consider if we are doing the work God planned for *us* and if He is ultimately getting the glory.

God often takes us into uncomfortable situations so people can meet Him through us. Yes, it can be scary but go anyway.

I have worked with volunteers as we stepped out of our comfort zones into the specific work God prepared for us. Our knees were wobbly but we trusted in the loving heart of our Father and He used us in ways we never would have dreamed or attempted on our own. We had all sorts of volunteer dinners and notes of encouragement and appreciation from the staff and board, which were great. But at the end of every shift, we prayed thanking God and giving Him the glory for the ministry and the lives touched that day (including ours). A great power for good is set loose in the world when our actions reflect and acknowledge the character of God.

For we are God's workmanship, created in Christ Jesus to do good works, which God prepared in advance for us to do.
Ephesians 2:10

❋ ❋ ❋

I sit in the same room with televised football quite a bit during that *very* long season. It's the only way to spend time with my family. I'm not always paying attention but it tickles me when I see a football player drop to one knee and point skyward, as he gives God credit for a touchdown. Now, even though both teams may pray before the game, I don't believe God favors one team over another. However, I bet He smiles when a Christian athlete visibly recognizes that his strength and ability to help the team comes from God.

As we go about our days, let's remember whose team we are on and who trains and equips us to play. The name of the team is Christian, the purpose is love and the outcome is good deeds toward our fellow players in the name of Jesus Christ our coach.

Not that we are adequate in ourselves to consider anything as coming from ourselves, but our adequacy is from God...
2 Corinthians 3:5 NASB

 Be a woman of integrity. Goodness will follow.

We need to ask God to help us be consistently honest and trustworthy. It feels a bit scary because it calls us to face up to some issues we would normally like to sidestep.

I love a good story and am prone to exaggerate to make it more interesting. The original story is always best. I've also been known to out-and-out lie. I became very adept at lying as a teenager and it was a difficult habit to overcome as an adult. The Holy Spirit has made me very sensitive to my tendencies in this area and usually brings me up short before I "add a little color" or tell a whopper.

You're not too sure what to do with someone prone to fibbing. What do you believe and what don't you believe? Lying destroys trust as well as our Christian witness. I got caught in a big lie in college and was lovingly confronted by the friends my dishonesty hurt. I was incredibly embarrassed, but they forgave me and kept on loving me. I wasn't a believer yet, but I think that was the beginning of my journey into understanding the joy and freedom of living and speaking the truth. When I came to Christ at thirty-four I learned that honesty is simply God's way.

Do not let kindness and truth leave you; bind them around your neck,
write them on the tablet of your heart. So you will find favor and good
repute in the sight of God and man.
Proverbs 3:3 NASB

In addition to this, God has shown me just because I think some-thing doesn't make it the truth. Even if I'm right, it's rarely appropriate (unless I come upon someone, really or figuratively, about to jump off a bridge) to hurt someone or hammer them with my opinion in the name of being honest. I must always be loving and considerate of other's feelings when I speak the truth or share an opinion.

I'm a mother-in-law and a grandma. I have lots and lots of knowl-edge and really helpful opinions which I'm sure are accurate because they exist in my head or were personal experiences. Unfortunately, speaking my version of the truth when my opinion wasn't asked for or wanted resulted in family tension and hurt feelings. I eventually learned to keep my big mouth shut. Even more humbling, my daughter-in law is a great mother without my help.

I'm trying to stick to being a good, supportive friend and grandma. Occasionally I'm blessed when she trusts me enough to ask for my advice.

The king rejoices when his people are truthful and fair.
Proverbs 16:13 TLB

He who guards his mouth and his tongue, guards his soul from troubles.
Proverbs 21:23 NASB

 Goodness chooses obedience.

How much good we do depends on how closely we listen to the Spirit and how quickly we choose to obey. The longer I wait to do something the Spirit is prompting the less likely I am to do it. As I go through my days, I make so many decisions I'm not even aware of them all. Some are big but most involve the little choices I face in my corner of the world. When I stay close to God through His word and prayer, and listen to and obey the promptings of the Holy Spirit in *all* my decisions, I'm headed straight on the Christian road. It hasn't happened yet, but I'm sure that's the case.

Unfortunately, I often feel like the old cartoon character with a devil on one shoulder and an angel on the other, both talking at once. How's a person to think! I know the angel is speaking truth but, sometimes, the devil sounds pretty good. If I'm not consciously, sometimes minute by minute, tipping my head toward the angel, listening for the voice of the Holy Spirit and acting accordingly, I'm going to be weaving all over that road. God won't let me fall in the ditch permanently, but it can be a long, painful journey if I listen to the wrong voice. Plus, all my energy and focus is aimed at damage control instead doing the good works God has prepared for me. When I refuse to stay on God's side of the road I'm not just useless to Him I'm a dangerous stumbling block to others. I lose my witness to unbelievers and my trust and credibility with my fellow Christians.

The devil is portrayed as tiny in cartoons. In reality he is a roaring lion and he certainly doesn't want me doing anything good for anyone, especially in the name of Jesus. He's no match for God but he knows the areas of my life where I'm a pushover and gives me a shove toward my weak spots every chance he gets.

Now, I'm aware of a lot of my weaknesses and, like a good Christian soldier, need to prepare my weapons in advance. I haven't been in the army but I know from listening to my Dad that obedience is crucial to a soldier's safety and effectiveness. If a soldier ignores a command and goes his own way, he is easy prey for the enemy and endangers the rest of the men. God has called us to an army that delivers the helpful, encouraging, sweet smelling fruit of goodness to a hurting world at war. If we aren't obedient He will not be able to use us for the good that needs doing or the wrong that needs righting. We need to make sure we are on God's side. We may stumble and get hit by a flaming arrow now and then but,

The LORD is my strength and my shield; My heart trusts in Him, and I am helped; Therefore my heart exults, and with my song I shall thank Him.

The LORD is their strength, and He is a saving defense to His anointed.
Psalm 28:7-8 NASB

He will pick us up, dust us off, and give us our marching orders. Your decision to obey, whether the issue is big or small, is of infinite importance.

My sheep listen to my voice; I know them, and they follow me.
John 10: 27

The fruit you bear shows who you are listening to—whose side you're on. So, fill your arms with the fruit of goodness and listen to the Spirit. He will guide you to the people who need what God wants you to give.

For I was hungry, and you gave Me something to eat; I was thirsty,
and you gave Me drink; I was a stranger and you invited Me in;
naked and you clothed Me; I was sick and you visited Me;
I was in prison, and you came to Me.
Then the righteous will answer Him, saying, 'Lord, when did we see
You hungry, and feed you, or thirsty, and give You drink? And when
did we see You a stranger, and invite You in, or naked, and clothe You?
And when did we see You sick, or in prison, and come to You?'
"And the King will answer and say to them, 'Truly I say to you,
to the extent that you did it to one of these brothers of Mine,
even the least of them, you did it to Me.
Matthew 25:35-40 NASB

Consider your attitude.

If we take our cue from the circumstances in the world and our personal lives, which often seem out of control, it's easy to be discouraged and negative, to have a "cup half empty" attitude. But, you know what? Your attitude is one of the few things you *can* control. I just heard you say, "No, I can't," but, "yes, you can!" Here's why.

In the world you have tribulation, but take courage;
I have overcome the world.
John 16:33

That's a "cup half full" statement if ever I heard one.

Following is the definition of "attitude" from Webster's New World Dictionary and Thesaurus with the word (good) added in front of each description to give you an idea of what I'm talking about. Here goes:

"1. A (good) bodily posture showing (good) mood, (good) action, etc., 2. a (good) manner showing one's (good) feelings or (good) thoughts, 3. a (good) disposition, (good) opinion, etc." Webster's thesaurus adds: "(good) reaction, (good) demeanor, (good) temperament, (good) frame of mind and (good) character."

God is writing a story in each of our lives with chapters on tribulation, courage and overcoming. Since you've read this far, you know that my story often includes struggles with my attitude. I tend to shift with fears and feelings, hurts and hunger, weight and weather...just about anything can affect my outlook on life. Rich says he can "feel" my attitude in the house when he comes home from work. Sometimes he probably wishes he could go back.

As I read back over John 16:33b and the definition of attitude with my (goods) inserted, I realized I *can* control how I see my particular cup of water. I'm a Christian. Jesus, the source of "living water," lives in me. I need to let a thirsty world see that my cup isn't half empty *or* half full. My cup overflows.

In the vast scheme of things my constant attitude changes don't amount to much. But in the tiny corner where my God has placed me, it does. It matters a lot. Unpredictable moods and a negative attitude can sour the sweet fruit of goodness.

Thou dost prepare a table before me in the presence of my enemies;
thou hast anointed my head with oil; my cup overflows.
Surely goodness and lovingkindness will follow me all the days of my life:
and I will dwell in the house of the LORD forever.
Psalm 23:5-6 NASB

"Ready position" for goodness sake.

When our grandson, Emitt, began playing baseball, his coach constantly reminded them, in a loud voice, to get into "ready position." Those who weren't kicking the dirt or gazing at the clouds would spread their legs, bend their knees, extend their arms for balance, lift their heads and look forward.

My knowledge of sports is limited so I asked Rich, "Why do they have to get in that position?"

"The coach is building an athletic foundation so they are able to move in any direction when, and if, the ball is hit toward them. Tennis, football, basketball, most all sports, have some version of "ready position," he explained with a hint of male superiority.

"Huh," I said. "Now I understand why the coach keeps yelling it at them. Too bad they don't do it. They rarely move even if they're *in* the right position."

"Well, those kids have a lot to try to remember and it takes practice," he said, probably remembering his own inept beginnings at baseball.

As the season wore on and we sat through seemingly endless games, I heard "ready position" hollered at those boys over and over. By the end of the season, which I thought would never come, they were getting in position without being told and were actually playing baseball. I was impressed.

"Hey," I said to Rich during the last game. "What if we could program our brains to be in "ready position" to respond to people's needs quickly when God sends the ball our way?"

"Sounds interesting," he said. I think he might have rolled his eyes.

"Let's see," I said, taking my notebook and pen out of my purse, "we would need to:

* Read our Bibles so we would have a strong foundation (feet on the ground). God's call on our lives would need to be our first priority.
* Pray, which would flex our knees, extend our arms and enable us to go and do the good works God plans for us. Even the unexpected or uncomfortable things.

- Keep our heads up to see the needs in our churches and communities and to hear the prompting of the Holy Spirit. This may require leaving a bit of wiggle room in our schedules so we have time and space to respond."

I finally stopped for air.

"You're quite the list maker," Rich said with a smile. "I agree, though. As Christians we do need to pay attention and get more involved in the game."

"To this end also we pray for you always that our God may count you worthy of your calling, and fulfill every desire for goodness and the work of faith with power in order that the name of our Lord Jesus may be glorified in you, and you in Him, according to the grace of our God and the Lord Jesus Christ."
2 Thessalonians 1:11-12 NASB

Goodness

Sharing Fruit

 Do the good that is needed.

Mom hit the ground hard. One minute we were walking and talking and in the space of two steps she was no longer beside me.

We were spending our annual weekend in Seaside on the Oregon coast and the weather was beautiful. There is a boardwalk where you can walk for miles without having to trudge through the soft sand to get to the ocean. Perfect for Mom. The boardwalk is actually a triple-wide concrete sidewalk with room for walkers, bicyclers, skateboarders, couples with strollers, dogs and joggers.

Mom and I were on our way back to our motel from the shops when Mom tripped over a raised section of cement. She fell face first skinning her knees, elbows, hands and chin. The fall knocked the wind out of her and she didn't move for a few seconds. Scared me half to death.

"Mom, are you hurt?" I asked, feeling a surge of panic, as I dropped to my knees beside her.

Finally, she looked at me with tears in her eyes and said, "No, honey, I'm okay. Just embarrassed."

I helped her to her feet and retrieved her packages she let fly when she tried to catch herself. As I turned around I saw a middle-aged couple sitting on a bench not ten feet away watching. Other walkers simply stepped around us.

Not one of those people offered help or asked if Mom was okay. I was shocked. Later, when I had time to think, I got mad. Mom wasn't seriously hurt but she could have been. They didn't know. Those people definitely failed the Good Samaritan test.

We made it, slowly, to the car then off to Safeway for bandages, hydrogen peroxide and antiseptic cream. Mom was emotionally shaken, her body jarred and achy, and her contact points bloody. She waited in the car.

"How are you feeling now?" I asked when I returned with the medical supplies.

"A bit shaken. I'd forgotten how bad skinned knees hurt. Mostly, I feel embarrassed to have fallen down in front of all those people. And look," she said lifting one of her legs, "I tore holes in the knees of my best pants."

I sympathized but kept my mouth shut about the people who watched the show and didn't lift a finger to help. I didn't want her to feel worse.

I decided, then and there, I don't ever want to be one of those "watchers." I don't want you to be one either. We are called to love our neighbor as ourselves, not to pass by when someone is lying in the middle of the sidewalk. We all fall down from time to time and need a helping hand to get back on our feet. James 3:2 says, "we all stumble in many ways."

Let's remember our own falls and be quick to come to the aid of our fellow stumblers. The Holy Spirit is not in the business of producing sitters and watchers. He wants people who make a difference.

In Luke 10:25-37, Jesus tells the parable of the Good Samaritan. I encourage you to read these verses. In verse 36, Jesus questions the lawyer who prompted the story when he asked, "And who is my neighbor?" in verse 29.

Jesus concluded the story by asking the lawyer, ""Which of these three do you think was a neighbor to the man who fell into the hands of robbers?" The expert in the law replied, "The one who had mercy on him." Jesus told him, "Go and do likewise."

 Be generous with what you have and who you are.

I don't want to belabor stories about my mother but she's the first person to come to mind when writing about goodness. Besides, she's been gone for fourteen years and I enjoy sharing memories.

Anyway, Mom had a rich Uncle Bob in Kansas who died and left his fortune to his sizable and widely disbursed family. Mom didn't receive vast sums but welcomed the unexpected checks that showed up from time to time. A year after the last check Mom assumed the estate had finally settled. Not quite. One more check appeared out of the blue with a letter informing her that this *was* the final check.

Mom called me and said, "Guess what? Uncle Bob just sent me more money. There's enough for Dad and me *and* you and Rich to buy new cars. What do you say?"

At the time we were cramming ourselves and two growing boys into a tiny Honda so we jumped for joy. With the trade-in on our car we were able to buy a new mini-van which served our family faithfully for many years.

Mom could have squirrelled that money away but I think she had more fun sharing it with us. No strings attached, no reminders of her generosity, just pleasure in our enjoyment of the new car.

Most of us don't have a rich Uncle Bob but we can still show goodness through the blessings God has provided. Money is always good but so is our time or our talent. How about the gift of a listening ear accompanied by a tender heart? Or vegetables from your garden? Maybe an offer to grocery shop or a ride to the store for an elderly neighbor.

Try to perform a simple good deed for someone every day (your family counts). Be creative. This is fun and can become addictive. If you have children or grandchildren, get them in on the act.

There is so much fruit in the basket God keeps filled to overflowing for us. Like loaves and fishes, there is always enough to go around and then some. Endless choices of good gifts to give with no strings, just love.

> *Let all that you do be done in love.*
> 1 Corinthians 16:14 NASB

> *If anyone has material possessions and sees his brother in need*
> *but has no pity on him, how can the love of God be in him?*
> *Dear children, let us not love with words or tongue*
> *but with actions and in truth.*
> 1 John 3:17-18

Ŏ Help people see the good you see in them.

Look for the best in others. We tend to find what we look for, good or bad, so keep your antenna up for the good. When you find it, say so. Give an honest compliment or express appreciation. Don't take the goodness of others for granted.

Most of us are quick to believe negative things about ourselves— we need to hear lots of positives. Can you remember a time when a kind word, a simple compliment or a genuine smile made your day?

When my daughter-in law was going through chemo and lost all her hair, we decided to go to Nordstrom's for make-overs. Without a wig or scarf she walked out into the world with her sweet bald head. The young man who waited on us didn't bat an eye. He asked her questions about her treatment and how she was feeling. Then he stood back and looked at her. Really looked.

"You don't need a make-over," he said softly. "You are absolutely beautiful just the way you are." He was right, of course, but he gave her words she needed to hear when he could have sold her a pile of make-up.

Of course, he made up for it when he got to me.

❋ ❋ ❋

As we go through our days we see so many good things that go unacknowledged.

- Beautiful worship at church or a sermon that touched or convicted us.
- Great service in a restaurant or well-behaved children at the next table.
- A delicious perfume or great hair style.
- Someone faithfully caring for an aging parent or handicapped child.
- Mothers with small children or teenagers.
- People who quietly serve behind the scenes.
- Elderly saints who have lived and served well.
- Missionaries.
- Children of all ages.
- Husbands, families and friends.

Show your appreciation through a personal comment, a handwritten note, an e-mail, a hug or even a thumbs-up—whatever is appropriate. Do it or say it right when you think of it or the moment will get lost in the world of good intentions. Don't forget new people God puts in your path. An honest, positive word from you may be the very thing they need to keep going. The words they need to see Jesus.

Do not withhold good from those to whom it is due,
when it is in your power to do it.
Proverbs 3:27 NASB

Show courtesy. Good manners are important.

I grew up in a world where my Mom put on a dress and gloves to go to the bank. My high school had a dress code which stated girls had to wear dresses and socks (which meant nylons with those horrible garter belts). I think there was even a brief season when we couldn't wear patent leather shoes so the boys (those rascals) couldn't see up our skirts. Sheesh! Boys were expected to tuck in their shirts and have short, combed hair-cuts. The teachers dressed in a professional manner. Sort of a *Leave it to Beaver* world. It didn't always work out that way but that was the idea.

I graduated in 1968—the year the dress code was lifted for students and staff. This wasn't a terrible thing and, at the time, I was upset I'd missed out. However, the lifting of social expectations coupled with the rebellious attitude that swept the nation during the Viet Nam War (I agreed and was part of it) began to morph into disrespect for authority and each other.

The women's movement (I agreed and was part of that, too) encouraged many needed reforms but also undermined the masculinity of our men and, in many ways our own femininity. Don't get me wrong. I support *most* women's rights but I think we shot ourselves in both feet when we no longer asked for simple manners and behavior from our men or required them of ourselves.

I'm part of the in-between generation. My adult jobs required professional clothes which helped me look like I knew what I was doing. I also needed to treat customers with respect and a smile (no matter what!) and couldn't chew gum on the job. For years I perfected my sense of balance by cramming myself into "control top" panty hose every morning before work. Rich found it very entertaining and called it my "stork dance."

My point is (what was my point?), oh yes. Manners are nice, considerate and a pleasure to give and receive. "Please" and "thank-you," an opened door, "excuse me," simple table etiquette, family and community traditions, appropriate telephone behavior...are refreshing and respectful. There are endless choices of good words, gestures and actions that demonstrate we care about each other and ourselves.

How many of the personal, community and even global problems that face our troubled world could be avoided or at least helped with the expectation and application of good conduct, personal responsibility and manners. Unfortunately, we are not born with a tendency toward particularly good behavior. We have to be taught. All of us, regardless of our age, need to cultivate good manners and teach others with our words and by example before we all forget.

As I approached the door to Macy's recently a young man with droopy pants exposing lime green underwear and those strange ear lobe expanders walked up beside me and quickened his pace. I thought of making a run for the door but he beat me to it and opened it for me with a smile. Hoping my apprehension didn't show, I smiled and thanked him as I entered the store. I knew this young man had a good mother.

I don't advocate outdated codes of conduct but we would all benefit by treating each other and being treated with respect, courtesy and a garnish of goodness (just no more panty hose, please!)

I know I've used this verse before, but I believe Jesus wasn't kidding when He told us:

> *Therefore, however you want people to treat you, so treat them,*
> *for this is the Law and the Prophets.*
> Matthew 7:12 NASB

Or, as Eugene Peterson paraphrases Matthew 7:12 in The Message:

Here is a simple, rule-of-thumb guide for behavior: Ask yourself what you want people to do for you, then grab the initiative and do it for them. Add up God's Law and Prophets and this is what you get.

Thank You!

Don't bury your talents. Use them to multiply the goodness of God.

I just finished reading Jesus' parable of the talents in Matthew 25 verses 14-30. The talents represent the gifts God gives each of us and the story describes how faithfully we use them for kingdom service. As followers of Christ we know His heart and intentions are loving and kind and we can use what we have been given for the good of His kingdom—unlike the man who buried his talents out of fear. We are all given gifts, abilities and talents. All different and all equally precious to God. We need to take personal responsibility for what we have been given and be productive in our own unique way.

The Spirit gives us "talents" to fit every occasion so we have no excuse to be indifferent to our gifts. The Fruit of the Spirit in Galatians 5:22-23 is just one example. Look at the love verses in 1 Corinthians 13:4-8 or the characteristics of Christian life in Colossians 3:5-17. Study Paul's words to the Romans in Romans 12:9-21. I recommend you read these verses then search the Scriptures yourself. The Bible is chock full of ways to use our talents to demonstrate the goodness of God to the world around us.

I can be lazy and tend to bury my "talents" so I don't lose them, thinking I'll get to them later (like a squirrel). I need to dig up what I've buried before I forget where and what it is and ask God to show me how to use all I have been blessed with. I need to respond to the incredible opportunity to bring the light of Christ's goodness to others.

There is so much darkness in the world. Sometimes I feel helpless and overwhelmed. But there is a mighty power darkness cannot conquer—the force of loving acts of goodness done in Jesus name.

I know I will make mistakes and miss opportunities along the way but, at the end of my journey, when I meet Jesus face to face, I so want to hear, "Well done, good and faithful servant!" (Matthew 25:21). Don't you?

...let your light shine before men, that they may see your good deeds
and praise your Father who is in Heaven.
Matthew 5:16

FRUIT FOR THOUGHT

Goodness

Nurturing Fruit

1. Can you think of a time when goodness was withheld or given for the wrong reasons? How about a time when goodness was given and God received the glory?

2. What does the word integrity mean to you? How does it look in your life?

3. What is your "gut" reaction to the word obedience? (I know, UGH!). How can your choice to be obedient or disobedient to God reflect goodness toward the lives around you? What do you think about my Dad's story about soldiers?

4. Do you feel you are in control of your attitude in your corner of the world? Make a list of the ways your "cup runs over."

5. What life changes would you need to make to be in "ready position" when God sends a goodness prompt in your direction?

Sharing Fruit

1. How did you react to the story of my Mom falling down? What would you have done if you were sitting on the bench?

2. In what ways (be creative here) could you share what you have and who you are with others? What do you think of the good deed a day idea?

3. List three (or more) practical things you could do this week to help others see the good you see in them.

4. How did you react to the section on manners? Your response may depend on your age but, hopefully, we can all agree with Matthew 7:12. It's helpful to look up the verse and write it out. What does it say to others when we demonstrate good manners?

5. What talents for good has God given you? Are you using them or burying them (or a little of both)? Write out Matthew 5:16 and put your name at the beginning.

❊ ❊ ❊

Grab your notebook and write out...

◆ One Scripture from this chapter that is particularly meaningful to you.

◆ Your Thoughts and Stories

❊ ❊ ❊

Chapter Seven

THE FRUIT OF THE SPIRIT IS ... FAITHFULNESS

Kathy, Liz and Frank

The church committee meeting had gone well followed by an open and genuine time of prayer. We were done early so decided to grab a quick lunch before going our separate ways. Over lunch we laughed, shared stories and, unfortunately, did a fair amount of griping about husbands, children, boyfriends and friends. We all participated in this familiar female activity, except Kathy.

I felt vaguely uncomfortable driving back to work and it didn't take any deep thinking to figure out why. My dear Christian sisters and I had come straight from a meeting and prayer time and jumped feet-first back into the world. Our conversation over lunch didn't sound much different from anyone else's. An eavesdropper (like God) would never have recognized us as nice, born-again, Christian ladies. We might not have cussed or been vulgar but everyone except Kathy had stepped over a God-line.

Later that day I called Kathy and we made a date for coffee at her office the next day.

"What's up?" she asked. "Are you going to give me a hint?"

"Nope, but give me your coffee order and I'll be there at 10:00."

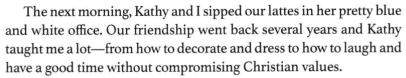

The next morning, Kathy and I sipped our lattes in her pretty blue and white office. Our friendship went back several years and Kathy taught me a lot—from how to decorate and dress to how to laugh and have a good time without compromising Christian values.

I was about to learn something new.

"Kathy, I've noticed you never share anything negative about Steve (her husband), or anyone else for that matter. I felt unsettled when I left lunch yesterday. Our conversation was often critical and some things were shared that sounded confidential. I know I said some inappropriate things just to get a laugh."

Kathy smiled at me but didn't say anything so I went on.

"I think Steve is great but I'm pretty sure he and the rest of the people in your life aren't perfect. You're making a choice the rest of us aren't. Will you tell me about it?"

Kathy thought for a moment then said, "Faithfulness."

"Okay," I said. "I need more."

"Being faithful to our husbands doesn't just mean not having an affair. Most of us would never dream of doing such a thing let alone have the time, energy or underwear. How we talk about our husbands to others is a very important aspect of faithfulness. It makes me sad when I hear anyone, especially a "nice" group of Christian women, verbally shred their husbands. It breaks our marriage vows to honor and respect and gives others a one-sided, negative impression of the men we claim to love. It also reinforces those things, which are usually trivial, in our own minds until eventually that's all we see. The same goes for our family, friends and children. I simply choose to be faithful."

Wow! That was quite a speech and I took every word to heart. God and Kathy gave me much to think about and raised the bar on my behavior.

❋ ❋ ❋

Liz and I were friends during Junior High. This proved to be a precarious time of life. I don't know all the challenges boys faced but girls faced the dangerous territory of each other. Friends one day and enemies the next, secrets shared and secrets told, cliques and cruelty, all part of a twelve-year-olds life. That was over fifty years ago but I don't imagine things have changed.

I remember hurts and tears. Friendships that made the rounds like musical chairs. I remember gossip and cruel laughter. I participated in my fair share.

Everyone liked Liz and yet she wasn't part of any clique or "in" crowd. Kind and generous, she was very sensitive to other people's feelings and never gossiped or talked badly about another person. She could be a little irritating at times when I really wanted to share something juicy because she didn't want to hear it, but I admired and trusted her. I knew that if she never spoke badly about anyone else with me, she didn't talk about me when she was with others. On top of that she was fun to be with.

I wasn't a Christian back then but Liz went to a church in our neighborhood. She often invited me to come with her but I never did. As I look back I see Liz as one of the steppingstones on my journey to becoming a Christian. I think she believed what the Bible said and lived her faith—not easy for a junior higher. I didn't realize it at the time but the Holy Spirit was alive and well in Liz and I wanted to be like her. I saw firsthand the fruit of faithfulness and tasted its goodness through her.

It took twenty-two years and many more steppingstones for God to get me to the cross. Liz probably doesn't know how He used her in my life but it was her faithfulness to the people in her world that began to create a longing to know the Source of that faithfulness for mine.

I lucked out in the in-law department when I married Rich. I loved Frank and Gretchen and they loved me. Not only were they kind to me but they were kind to each other. Frank was a good provider with that post-depression work ethic and Gretchen came close to being a Proverbs 31 woman. They passed these qualities down to Rich and David, their boys, who became good, faithful husbands and fathers.

Gretchen was diagnosed with inoperable cancer when our second son, James, was a year old. She didn't want to go through chemotherapy for a few extra months of life so went home to a hospital bed in the dining room. Frank stepped uncomplaining into the role of caretaker. Gretchen had always managed the house and money so he learned to do all those things, and do them well, so she wouldn't worry. He chose the hard side of faithfulness because of the soft side of his love for his wife.

Frank never complained as he cleaned and cared for all Gretchen's personal needs. He tempted her with food she wouldn't eat and sat at her bedside and watched game after game of baseball—her new-favorite sport. She loved the detail of keeping player stats and he helped her continue when she was too weak to write.

He stayed by the side of the woman he loved the night the intensity of her pain sent them to the hospital. He held her hand as she died. Frank stayed the course and I saw faithfulness lived out in one of life's hardest realities.

Faithfulness

Nurturing Fruit

🍎 **Consider God's faithfulness.**

Rich and I became Christians as adults. We can each look back and see God's faithful, guiding hand in all the "before" years and in our continuing journey as followers of Christ.

We used to think religion was a crutch weak people needed to lean on. A story people needed to make sense of the world and their lives. While we mocked Christians and "organized religion," God faithfully placed His people and circumstances in our lives. People and circumstances that would ultimately guide each of us on our winding paths to the cross. We did not come to Jesus at the same time but when we became a Christian couple, we realized those mocking words of our youth were actually true, just not in the critical way we intended. In our weakness and sin Jesus provided the only "crutch" strong and faithful enough to hold us. The story of the cross and Christ's faithful life and sacrificial death was written for us. Our salvation through faith in Christ became the only belief that made sense of our lives.

Now, when we hear individuals ridicule our faith or our culture criticize Christians, we stop and wonder what God is up to as His great faithfulness continues to move stones away from hardened hearts.

Has the hand of God placed you or me at a strategic point in someone else's journey to the cross?

I will praise you, O Lord, among the nations; I will sing of you among the peoples. For great is your love, reaching to the heavens; your faithfulness reaches to the skies.
Psalm 57:9-10

🍎 Be faithful to God.

I'm one of those people who consistently shows up right on time or even a bit early. Dentist appointments, meetings, parties, babysitting grandkids, dinner with the girls, even my colonoscopy—I'm right on time. I would love to say this is because I'm a really conscientious person but it's more about feeling self-conscious walking into a crowded room, fear of disapproval and a desire to feel in control.

I keep something to read in my car to entertain myself when I'm twenty minutes early wherever I'm expected to be.

The one time my faithful, on-time habit fails me, though, is with Jesus. The Mary in me longs to spend quiet, undisturbed time with Him, "listening to the Lord's word, seated at His feet" (Luke 10:39 NASB). I know He is waiting patiently for me to put in an appearance but often the Martha in me takes over and I hit the ground running and let my to-do list rule my day.

Martha, Martha (Annie, Annie) you are worried and bothered about so many things; but only a few things are necessary, really only one, for Mary has chosen the good part, which shall not be taken away from her.
Luke 10:41-42 NASB

The good news is, God loves me, He knows me, and he gently but persistently continues to call me into His presence. He wants to be with me! How incredible is that? So now we have an appointment time. Sometimes I'm late and some days I don't show up at all, but most of the time I'm early and I don't have to wait in the car.

God speaks to me and calms my heart and mind through His Word as He teaches me to listen. He patiently hears my prayers and tolerates my helpful instructions (I'm trying to quit offering so many suggestions but I remind Him that He did, after all, make me a female).

Sometimes I can almost see Him sitting on the couch in Khaki pants drinking a cup of coffee. Other times I hear His voice so clearly through His Word it takes my breath away. Some days are quiet and soft, other days powerful and convicting. Then there are simple faith days when I don't sense His presence at all, but I know He's there and He wants me there too.

As I grow older, the pull of the world and my to-do list is beginning to fade and the longing to spend time with my God is growing stronger. My Martha is beginning to relax and sit still next to my Mary. I wish she'd figured this out a long time ago! I'm showing up on a pretty regular basis for our appointments and we're getting together informally almost all the time.

God's steady presence and my response to Him is growing the fruit of faithfulness in my life.

The LORD is near to all who call on him, to all who call on him in truth.
Psalm 145:18

Let love and faithfulness never leave you; Bind them around your neck,
Write them on the tablet of your heart.
Proverbs 3:3

🍎 Faithful communion with Jesus.

One of the rites of passage I experienced as a new believer was participating in communion. The church I attended had communion once a month and I remember the unexpected tears the first time I was able to receive the bread and wine (a.k.a. grape juice) with the rest of the believers. I belonged to Jesus. I belonged to the body of Christ—His body. Since that day I have always anticipated and enjoyed taking communion. I long to bring a spanky-clean version of Annie to Jesus but, unfortunately, that Annie doesn't exist, except by the grace of God. It is only by His amazing grace that I am able to partake of the bread and wine and be cleansed by the body and blood they represent. The now familiar words will never grow old.

... The Lord Jesus, on the night he was betrayed, took bread, and when he had given thanks, he broke it, and said, 'This is my body, which is for you; do this in remembrance of me.' In the same way, after supper he took the cup, saying, 'This cup is the new covenant in my blood; do this, whenever you drink it, in remembrance of me.'
1 Corinthians 11:23-25

The disciples sitting around that long-ago Passover table didn't understand Jesus' words until after His crucifixion. We came to faith in Christ on the other side of the cross and are able to receive Jesus' profound message to His disciples and all who would follow later. "Do this in remembrance of me."

You may be wondering what this has to do with nurturing faithfulness or if Annie is off on a rabbit trail. Let me hop back on the path.

One Sunday after communion, I visited with my friend Nancy as we headed out the sanctuary door. She is a tiny red-head, not quite five feet tall, but she possesses gigantic faith. She looked up at me and spoke words that took me to that upper room and into the heart of Jesus.

"When Pastor reads Jesus' words, "Do this in remembrance of me," she said with a soft smile, "I hear Jesus say, 'Don't forget me, Nancy.'"

"Don't forget me, Annie."

Communion has never been the same. Jesus asked me to remember Him. Not just the first Sunday of the month but every minute, every hour of every day for as long as I live. In all I do, all I say, all I think, and all I feel...remember. Do not forget Jesus.

That's eating the bread and drinking the wine of faithfulness.

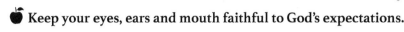 **Keep your eyes, ears and mouth faithful to God's expectations.**

We live in a world of information. Television and social media bombard our brains with more data than we are able to compute. I'm not sure God designed us to mentally or emotionally handle the detailed disasters, social gossip, world events and the infinite amount of information available to us. Throw in TV, movies, music, books and the general background noise of our environment and it's a wonder we can function at all. But we do. We may feel stressed and overwhelmed but we are also fascinated and sometimes addicted.

Many of the information and entertainment options available are excellent, some not worthy of our time or attention and some downright horrible. We aren't dumb, (although when I read the list of the most popular TV shows I sometimes wonder) and are quite capable of filtering out the "yuck" from our viewing and listening pleasure. So let's do it. Information and noise overload aren't what I really want to discuss here but they do fill our time and our brains with excess baggage that interferes with our faithfulness to God and others, so I thought it worth mentioning.

*The eye is the lamp of the body. If your eyes are good, your whole body
will be full of light. But if your eyes are bad, your whole body will be
full of darkness. If then the light within you is darkness,
how great is that darkness!*
Matthew 6:22-23

My biggest concern is what we do with the information in the smaller world we live in. Not the nightly news but the juicy tidbit we know about a friend and are dying to blab. Nothing that would show up on a google search but a sore spot in a relationship we would rather complain about than pray about. Not a TV show we know we shouldn't watch but eyes that look for weakness and imperfection in others and then the mouth that reports and passes judgment. I can write about this because I'm guilty as charged and God wants me to mend my ways.

Gossip, slander, sharing personal feelings designed to make another look bad, spreading strife, the list is long and the temptation great. I have heard gossip on the phone and slander over coffee. I have seen conflict and hurt between friends, within marriages and families, even within the church when inappropriate words and feelings are shared. I have participated in prayer groups where private information about someone not present was divulged in the form of a prayer request. When we look for faults and rehearse them in our minds and to others, they grow magnified and out of proportion. I'm sure you know what I'm talking about. But there is a better way.

Remember Kathy, who could have participated in "husband bashing" during lunch, but didn't? I wanted to know why. She *chose* to be faithful.

Remember Liz, who didn't listen to or repeat gossip? I admired and trusted her. She *chose* to be faithful.

Remember Frank, who served his dying wife without complaining? I watched a man live out his love. He *chose* to be faithful.

It is very easy for me to be unfaithful. It seems to satisfy a dark need within me. A need to fill my inadequacies, strike back at hurt, feel superior and righteous. I have been the grown-up version of the tattle-tale on the playground or the little girl chanting, "I know something you don't know," to her friends. I've also learned to be subtle in my unfaithfulness. Most of us have.

I encourage you to search the Word for God's specific message to you. I believe if we make a deliberate choice and ask God to help us look for the good in people and situations we will begin to think differently. As our thoughts change, so will our words and actions. It can be a long process but God is faithful and wants us to be faithful too.

There are so many Scriptures about what we see and think and say and do I can't begin to list them all. I decided on Paul's words to the Philippians because I believe they show the heart of faithfulness. If we truly internalize and begin to live these beautiful words, a faithful life will surely follow.

Finally, brothers, whatever is true, whatever is noble, whatever is right,
whatever is pure, whatever is lovely, whatever is admirable—if anything
is excellent or praiseworthy—think about such things.
Philippians 4:8

🍎 Faithful people don't sit on the sidelines.

*Whatever you have learned or received or heard from me, or seen
in me—put it into practice. And the God of peace will be with you.*
Philippians 4:9

Faithfulness is an action word. You can't demonstrate faithfulness
if you don't get off the couch and get going. You may love and memorize Paul's beautiful words (above) but never put them into practice.
If they are a nice greeting card sentiment or an interesting theory, we
have missed the message. I know from experience the couch is comfortable and reading about putting my faith into action *almost* feels
like I'm doing something—and I am—I'm sitting and reading. God
wants me to take the next step. Convert what I've learned into action.
Well, there goes the comfortable couch!

Please don't think I'm discouraging you from reading your Bible or
Christian books (after all I'm writing one). Good novels and non-fiction
are great too. We just need to take the next step and be "doers." Most of us
have enough information to respond and obey God's call to faithfulness
when we hear it. Of course we are to keep learning and growing deeper in
our faith but, right now, go with what you know. God will fill in the blanks.

Several years ago God called me to a season of life that was so far
out of my comfort zone I couldn't see it anymore.

"You can't be serious, I can't do that," I told Him.

Let me mention, this isn't a smart thing to say to God. I gave Him
really good excuses why He must be mistaken but He had me right
where He wanted me.

At the time I was studying the book of Deuteronomy with a group
of friends. From the following verses (and many more), you can see
why my arguments didn't get very far:

God said to Moses, "You have circled this mountain long enough. Now
turn north..." (2:3). "For the LORD your God has blessed you in all that
you have done; He has known your wanderings through this great wilder-
ness. These forty years the LORD your God has been with you; you have
not lacked a thing" (2:7). "So you shall observe to do just as the LORD your
God has commanded you; you shall not turn aside to the right or to the

left" (5:32). "For this commandment which I command you today is not too difficult for you, nor is it out of reach" (30:11). "Be strong and courageous, do not be afraid or tremble at them, for the LORD your God is the one who goes with you. He will not fail you or forsake you" (31:6 NASB).

God looked right into my chicken heart and provided everything I needed to perform the job at hand. The experience was a faith-walk for me all the way but I learned to trust God at a deeper level. I remained faithful because God did not fail me or forsake me.

Faithfulness comes in many shapes and sizes but, ultimately, the results are the same. God's people listening for God's call, obeying His commands, relying on His promises and staying the course.

But prove yourselves doers of the word, and not merely hearers who
delude themselves. For if anyone is a hearer of the word and not a doer,
he is like a man who looks at his natural face in a mirror;
for once he has looked at himself and gone away,
he has immediately forgotten what kind of person he was.
But one who looks intently at the perfect law,
the law of liberty, and abides by it,
not having become a forgetful hearer but an effectual doer,
this man shall be blessed in what he does.
James 1:22-25 NASB

Faithfulness

Sharing Fruit

🍎 **Faithfully maintain the relationships within the circle of your responsibility.**

The word "maintain" is derived from the Latin meaning "hold in the hand." Isn't that a beautiful word picture for the importance of the people God puts in our lives? How would we demonstrate faithfulness to someone precious God has placed in our cupped hands?

Webster's definition helps with the answer. "1. To keep or keep up; carry on. 2. To keep...in a state of repair. 3. To affirm... 4. To support by providing what is needed." The thesaurus added more helpful verbs, "preserve, keep, renew, care for, stick to and stand by."

Take a look at your cupped hands. Who's in there? Not the whole world (that's in God's hands) but a select few who touch our lives. We are personally responsible for each one at the point our lives intersect. Our parents and family, husbands and children, friends, employers, casual acquaintances, and our animals deserve to be loved and cared for in whatever way is appropriate. Some are with us for a lifetime, some for a season and some are simple, brief encounters. In many cases the responsibility is a two-way street and in others, one way. Whatever the case, streets need to be maintained. The road of faithfulness can be rough and potholes need repair before our tires go flat.

We are not designed to busily cram more and more into our cupped hands until, overwhelmed, we throw our arms in the air sending everyone and everything flying. No, we are meant to faithfully look into our hands and invest ourselves in who and what God gives us.

Each one should use whatever gift he has received to serve others,
faithfully administering God's grace in its various forms.
1 Peter 4:10

🍎 **Be where you are to be faithful to those who are with you.**

There are so many things in our culture (probably everyone's culture) that encourage us to isolate from each other. Attention stealers that allow us to *be there* and *not there* at the same time. Phones (texting, e-mailing or actually talking) are wonderful devices but often pull our attention away from the world around us. Being overly absorbed in a book, the newspaper, our computers and iPads, television, hobbies... anything that sucks us in and creates a force field around us effectively gives the people in our lives the message, "I am not available." We shut other people and even God out of our lives.

There is nothing wrong with any of these activities, and there are times we shouldn't be interrupted and deserve and need time to ourselves. But it's important to remember we live in community and the people around us are very special—to us and to God. Part of being faithful in our relationships is to be aware of the people around us and create a balance between "your time," "our time," and "my time." And, never forget that it's all "God's time."

There is an appointed time for everything. And there is a time
for every event under heaven—
Ecclesiastes 3:1 NASB

🍎 Show up.

Several years ago a friend told me her pastor's motto for life was, "Pray, do your homework, and show up." This simple thought on how to faithfully walk out the Christian life stuck with me all these years. What does this look like?

First, pray for the people involved in any given situation and ask God for His guidance. Second, look at the facts and do some research so you have an accurate knowledge of what is going on and what needs to be done, and finally, show up and do your part.

Back in my pre-Christian days, I based my response to invitations or life situations that needed action on how I felt. Sometimes I responded and sometimes I didn't. My standard comment to someone in need was, "Call me if you need anything." No one ever called and I knew they wouldn't but I felt virtuous for offering. Life was all about me—until I realized it wasn't.

Shortly after I became a Christian, my mother-in-law died. The service was held at a funeral home. The family was in a separate room off to the side of the chapel and we couldn't see the people who came to pay their respects to Gretchen and the family.

We held up pretty well during the funeral but came undone when we walked outside and saw the faces in the crowd. Of course Frank and Gretchen's friends were there, but so were ours. Rich's high school and college buddies and friends from work stood outside in

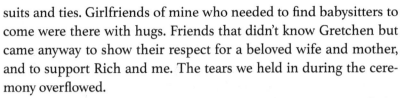
suits and ties. Girlfriends of mine who needed to find babysitters to come were there with hugs. Friends that didn't know Gretchen but came anyway to show their respect for a beloved wife and mother, and to support Rich and me. The tears we held in during the ceremony overflowed.

The same thing happened when Rich's dad died. Almost all the dear people I worked with came and extra chairs had to be added in the lobby. Once again we were incredibly blessed by the support shown our family. People took time out of their busy schedules to demonstrate their love and support by the simple act of being there.

I began to learn the power of showing up. The realization dawned. My response or attendance or reply or action should not be determined by my feelings, schedule or comfort level. Gifts, cards, phone calls, food or flowers are always appropriate and appreciated but, long after the gifts and cards are put away, the phone call ends, the food is eaten and the flowers fade, people will remember that you were there.

We are called to rejoice with others. If someone thought enough of me to invite me to their wedding or a baby shower or Tupperware party they deserve a response and, if possible, my attendance. I don't know how many times I have gone to a shower or get-together or Bible study and been so grateful I went as only three other people attended. Other times I enjoyed being part of a large group, added my presence to the event and had fun. Either way, I did my part and always came away blessed. People need people to fill the room and share their happiness and buy their Tupperware. It's not much of a party if nobody comes.

We are also called to weep with others. When someone we know, or is close to someone we know dies, find out when the service is, put on church clothes and go. In addition to attending, or if circumstances prevent us from going, send a card and give to a favorite charity in their name.

If someone is in the hospital, pick up a card and something you think they would like (flowers, magazines, jelly beans, whatever...) and visit. Pray for God to guide the timing of your visit and your focus. Call ahead, if possible, and ask if it's a good time for the patient. Don't tell them the gory details of your Aunt Selma's surgery and don't stay too long! Do your homework here. Find out exactly what is wrong and if it is serious or terminal. Sometimes your presence, with or without words, is all that is needed. However, be sensitive. Sometimes your presence isn't needed. People may want to be alone or just with family members. If that's the case, send a nice card and check back with them later and don't forget to pray.

Grieving family members, care givers, hurting friends, single moms, the elderly, people in rehab or nursing homes, the lonely... there are so many hurting people who need someone to simply visit or call. Someone safe to cry with, someone to listen, someone to truly care. Maybe even someone to gripe at. Don't assume somebody else is meeting the need. Wounded people need a touch from God and we may be the ones to give it.

We can't attend everything or visit everyone but, if we pray, the Holy Spirit will show us where we are needed. Then, however God guides us, show up.

Rejoice with those who rejoice; mourn with those who mourn.
Romans 12:15

🍎 Be committed to faithfulness.

My son and husband were recently discussing Rich's Fantasy football team (we won't go there). James gave Rich some advice and Rich said, "That's easy for you to say, you don't have any skin in the game."

"What's skin in the game?" I asked. I am a bottomless well of ignorance to both of them, but Rich humored me.

"It means James doesn't have anything to lose because he doesn't have any money invested in the game."

"Oh, and how much skin do you have in the game?" I asked suspiciously.

"Not much and this is the last year I'm going to have a team," he replied, trying to look innocent and not incite a mini-sermon.

He lucked out because the phrase got me thinking.

If you have read this far, I'm assuming you have made a commitment to Jesus. In doing so, you also made a commitment to His people. If we are not faithful in our commitment to God's people, He's going to notice. We've got skin in the game.

This is going to cost us but if we want Christ to be visible in our lives we need to ante up (sorry for the gambling analogies). Our time, our money, our comfortable lifestyle may be asked of us if we are truly committed to faithful service. Now, we can say we're committed and then sit back and do nothing. We might fool people for a short time but God sees us for what we are—complacent, lukewarm Christians unwilling to invest in the Kingdom.

We need to commit and act. The level of our action shows the depth of our faithfulness and commitment to God and His people. This may sound a bit scary but there is a beautiful passage in Isaiah that makes it clear what the world needs and what God expects from you and me. Look for the blessings.

> *Is this not the fast which I chose,*
> *To loosen the bonds of wickedness,*
> *To undo the bands of the yoke,*
> *And to let the oppressed go free,*
> *And break every yoke?*
> *Is it not to divide your bread with the hungry,*
> *And bring the homeless poor into the house;*
> *When you see the naked, to cover him;*
> *And not to hide yourself from your own flesh?*
> *Then your light will break out like dawn,*
> *And your recovery will speedily spring forth;*
> *And your righteousness will go before you;*
> *The glory of the LORD will be your rear guard.*
> *Then you will call, and the LORD will answer;*
> *You will cry and He will say, "Here I am."*
> *If you remove the yoke from your midst,*
> *The pointing of the finger, and speaking wickedness,*
> *And if you give yourself to the hungry,*

And satisfy the desire of the afflicted,
Then your light will rise in the darkness,
And your gloom will become like midday.
And the LORD will continually guide you,
And satisfy your desire in scorched places,
And give strength to your bones;
And you will be like a watered garden,
And like a spring of water whose waters do not fail.
And those from among you will rebuild the ancient ruins;
You will raise up the age-old foundations;
And you will be called the repairer of the breach,
The restorer of the streets in which to dwell.
Isaiah 58:6-12 NASB

This passage isn't for wimps or un-invested Christians. But what a beautiful call to faithfulness and commitment to God's people and what incredible promises of God's blessing in return.

🍎 The sparkle of faithfulness.

Like multi-faceted diamonds, faithful people sparkle. I have reached an age (well past middle) to have seen a lot of sparkly people. There are a variety of words that describe faithfulness and I have witnessed many people shining like stars as they do their part for the real people and circumstances God has given them. I wanted to name names and tell all the individual stories I know, but this book would never end. Besides, you have your own list of names, your own stories.

✳ ✳ ✳

The movie Camelot with Richard Harris and Vanessa Redgrave is my all-time favorite. Yes, it's about adultery and betrayal but it's also about love and faithfulness and forgiveness. At the end of the movie Sir Lancelot rescues Guenevere from being burned at the stake and England is about to go to war with France.

King Arthur is looking out over the camp the night before the battle begins when a young boy, Tom, who stowed away to fight for Camelot,

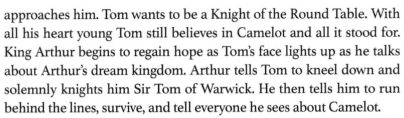

approaches him. Tom wants to be a Knight of the Round Table. With all his heart young Tom still believes in Camelot and all it stood for. King Arthur begins to regain hope as Tom's face lights up as he talks about Arthur's dream kingdom. Arthur tells Tom to kneel down and solemnly knights him Sir Tom of Warwick. He then tells him to run behind the lines, survive, and tell everyone he sees about Camelot.

King Arthur's old friend, King Pellinore, sees the boy and asks, "Who was that, Arthur?"

"One of what we all are, Pelly. Less than a drop in the great blue motion of the sunlit sea. But it seems some of the drops sparkle, Pelly. Some of them *do* sparkle."

Then the king turns in Tom's direction and yells, "Run boy, run. Run."

Now I've made myself cry.

Our kingdom isn't Camelot—it's far better. It's the Kingdom of God and the King, amid the vast sea of all He has created, sees us sparkle, and wants us to faithfully tell His story with our words and with our lives.

...shine like stars in the universe as you hold out the word of life...
Philippians 2:15-16

FRUIT FOR THOUGHT

Faithfulness

Nurturing Fruit

1. Describe God's faithfulness in your life. Can you see where He is using you as a stepping stone on someone else's journey to the cross?

2. Are you keeping a daily appointment with God or does your "to-do" list interfere? How could you adjust your schedule so the most important thing (faithful time with God) becomes a priority in your life?

3. What do you think about Jesus' specific call to "remember Him" in communion? How would this focus cultivate faithfulness in your life?

4. How does the information you take in from the world around you affect your faithfulness to others? In your smaller world, list three ways you have been unfaithful. Now, list what you can change to be faithful in those areas.

5. Have you ever tried to ignore God's call on your life or in a particular situation? How did that work for you? When you have been faithful to God's call (even if you felt chicken-hearted) what happened?

Sharing Fruit

1. Who are the people in your circle of responsibility? Does it change your perspective to realize God has placed them in your cupped hands? How can you faithfully maintain or provide what is needed for each life that intersects yours? Long term? For a season? Brief encounters? Critters?

2. What activities in your life tend to isolate you from others? What do others do that makes you feel isolated? How does this tendency toward isolation impact faithfulness in relationships?

3. How would you live out, "pray, do your homework and show up?" Give examples.

4. Do you have "skin in the game" in your commitment to God's people? What do you think about the statement, "the level of our action shows the depth of our faithfulness?" Does this sound like works or response?

5. Have you known or seen people who "sparkle" in their faithfulness? What makes them different? In what ways do you sparkle and how do others respond?

❄ ❄ ❄

Grab your notebook and write out...

♦ One Scripture from this chapter that is particularly meaningful to you.

♦ Your Thoughts and Stories

❄ ❄ ❄

Chapter Eight

THE FRUIT OF THE SPIRIT IS … GENTLENESS

The Doctor/Nurse Jenny

The Doctor

After seeing several doctors for a suspected hernia I ended up in the office of a real charmer. He was accompanied by two students one of whom originally brought me into the exam room. No instructions were given and no gown provided…just, "Wait here, the doctor will be in soon."

When the doctor came in he said, "Well, you're going to have to take your pants off if you want me to examine you. I can't see through 'em." I climbed off the exam table and took off my shoes and pants, then climbed back on feeling awkward and embarrassed in front of these three onlookers. The doctor proceeded to poke and prod around. I lay there mortified and getting angrier by the minute.

"I can't find anything, girlie," he said harshly, "but I'll send you for an ultrasound just in case." He turned around and abruptly left the room.

"*Girlie*?" I should have challenged him but didn't. Who did this guy think he was?

The students followed but the female of the two turned around at the door and whispered, "Sorry about that," and rolled her eyes. Apparently this behavior wasn't unusual.

It would have been so simple for the doctor to behave like a gentleman, medical and office procedures to be properly practiced, and the patient (me) be treated with respect and sensitivity. The whole fiasco could have been a totally different experience.

Webster's New World Dictionary states the opposite of gentleness as "roughness, harshness and imperviousness." This doctor received 100 percent.

Compare his story to the next one:

Nurse Jenny

"Annie, before we go to that *%#^$ hospital, run out and pick a bag of nice tomatoes for Jenny. If there are enough for a good mess of beans, pick those too...oh, and throw in a couple of cukes," Dad ordered from his recliner.

"Good idea Dad. Jenny will like that." I saluted as I grabbed a plastic bag and headed out the back door.

Since his last catheter change Dad talked incessantly about this produce delivery to Jenny. She is the only nurse he will see at the Urology Clinic. If Jenny isn't there, we turn around and go home.

During his last visit Jenny listened attentively as Dad told her about the crops he produces from his 50 x 100 foot city lot. They compared gardening tips as Jenny removed the old catheter tube which was inserted directly into Dad's bladder through his lower abdomen. She then cleaned the opening and inserted a new tube. The tube emptied into a bag which Rich and I changed twice a day.

"There you go, Mr. Smith, good as new. You stay out of trouble till next month."

"The tomatoes should be ripe by then, at least the Early Girls. Would you like me to bring you a few?" Dad asked.

"I would love some," Jenny smiled at Dad as she took his arm and led him to the waiting room.

Jenny never failed to give me a hug and a whispered word of encouragement as she handed Dad off. "Hang in there. You're doing a great job," or "One day at a time, he needs you."

Dad's relationship with Jenny began after his most recent brain surgery for a benign but aggressive tumor that continued to plague him after forty years. Dad was sent home from the hospital with a catheter and we began our regular trips to the Urology Clinic. Jenny saw him on his first visit. She took the time to explain what she was doing and engage my father in conversation.

Dad's face was disfigured from repeated surgeries and he lost an eye to the tumor years ago. Jenny always looked directly into his face and spoke to *him*—not to me as many of the doctors did. She *saw* my Dad as a person and treated him with respect and a firm gentleness.

Jenny was well aware of Dad's temper. She had seen him in action in the waiting room. She also knew he was embarrassed and frightened. He would begin to calm down when he saw her walk through the double doors to get him for his appointment.

"Mr. Smith, it's good to see you. Come on, I want to hear what you've been up to."

Dad would grumble and tell her about those *&%$# doctors that got him into this mess. Pretty soon they were chatting and sometimes I could hear Jenny laugh at Dad's gruff humor.

When Dad needed the catheter inserted directly into his bladder, Jenny explained it all to Dad and me and stayed with him during the procedure. In the weeks that followed Jenny encouraged and commiserated with Dad. She talked him down when he was frustrated and angry while, at the same time, validated his feelings. Her soft and gentle spirit combined with a no-nonsense approach deflated Dad's anger and threw him a lifeline of dignity and value and the knowledge that he was loved and cared for. She blessed Rich and me time and again with her compassion and support.

The third call I made when Dad died early the following year was to Jenny. I thanked her for the exceptional care and attention she gave a grumpy old man and his family and for showing me the power of gentleness in action.

Webster's defines gentleness as, "kindly, patient, tender, sensitive..." Webster would have been proud of Jenny. I'm sure God was.

Gentleness

Nurturing Fruit

 **Remember God's gentleness.**

The lights dimmed for the opening scene from Disney's movie *Planes*. It was my three-year-old grandson, Garrison's, first trip to the theater. He was excited but a bit nervous about the dark. He needn't have worried because as soon as the lights dimmed he fell asleep. Unfortunately, he wasn't heavy enough to hold the seat down and it slowly folded up on him as he relaxed. I reached over and pulled him onto my lap.

Garrison snuggled onto my chest and tucked his head under my chin. I slid down in my seat, my hands holding his bottom so he wouldn't slide to the floor. I would put my hand over his exposed ear when the action grew loud. He slept through the whole movie.

Total trust from him, a firm but gentle hold and unconditional love from me.

I wonder if this is how God feels when we step away from the noise and action of our world and curl up in His lap. Does He kiss the top of our heads and comfort us when the noisy world disturbs us?

Of course I know the answer. We are His children and are safe and secure in the gentle safety of His arms. We just need to recognize our need and let Him hold us.

Come to me, all you who are weary and burdened, and I will give you rest. Take my yoke upon you and learn from me, for I am gentle and humble in heart, and you will find rest for your souls. For my yoke is easy and my burden is light.
Matthew 11:28-29

🍉 **Practice being gentle with people.**

On a recent trip to the store shopping for a new curling iron, I picked out the one I wanted and tossed it in the cart. I continued down my shopping list which included light bulbs and eggs. As I gently laid these items in the basket being careful not to crush them, a light came on in my head (sorry about the pun). The curling iron was made of some kind of metal which could have withstood an armored assault and yet it was packaged in heavy cardboard and impenetrable thick plastic. I'm sure people have become violent or had breakdowns attempting to gain access to such items.

On the other hand, the delicate eggs and light bulbs were packed in flimsy cardboard. The eggs could easily come open and fall out or be crushed by setting the kitty litter on top of them (personal experience). The light bulb packages are open on both ends inviting disaster. I cannot begin to explain this marketing strategy except to say it defies logic. Although I suppose if eggs and light bulbs were packed like curling irons we would smash them anyway trying to get them open. There needs to be a middle ground here. It's a confusing world.

This experience, of course, led to a spiritual application. I have met a few people who appear to be packaged like curling irons. I don't believe that's who they really are, they have just been hurt or traumatized by people and circumstances and encased themselves in a hard shell to avoid being hurt again. They are fragile eggs and light bulbs on the inside.

The rest of us don our flimsy cardboard protection and bravely (or naively) step out to face the world. Well, people and life experiences being what they are, we all get cracked and shattered from time to time. Our shells leak and our lights won't shine. Sometimes we even fall out of our boxes completely.

We are all easily bruised and broken. We need to be very careful with each other, including, maybe especially, the people who appear to have hard shells. This isn't easy as we may have been cracking eggs for a long time. We will need to practice gentleness—regardless of our own hurt feelings or provocation. Let's start looking at one another as fragile beings. God's breakable people. Remember the nursery rhyme, Humpty Dumpty?

> *"Humpty Dumpty sat on a wall. Humpty Dumpty had a great fall.*
> *All the King's horses and all the King's men,*
> *Couldn't put Humpty Dumpty together again."*

Fortunately, we have a King who *can* put broken people back together again but I think He would prefer we be gentle in our words and actions and not crack each other in the first place.

I think the apostle Paul sums it up nicely in 1 Thessalonians 2:7.

> *...but we were gentle among you, like a mother caring*
> *for her little children.*

P.S. I've always suspected Humpty was pushed.

🍉 Horse Sense – a lesson on gentleness.

When our boys, Matt and James, started kindergarten and preschool my mornings were free three days a week. Rich, knowing my childhood dream of owning a horse, treated me to horseback riding lessons. I shared a horse with a teenage girl. It was a great arrangement. I could ride during the week and have my lesson and she did the same on the weekends. Our horse, Speck, was an aging Appaloosa who had been a competitive barrel racer in her prime.

Speck was a master at the art of "show not tell." I learned much more than how to saddle, bridle and ride a horse. She showed me gentleness. I know some people may object to giving human characteristics to animals but I've often seen better behavior from God's critters than from His children. Speck possessed a gentle heart, there's no other way to explain it.

She carefully lifted each hoof into the palm of my hand as I dug out the muck with a little pick before and after a ride. She stood perfectly still when I saddled her and she was so cooperative I think she would have bridled herself, if possible, just to save me the trouble. She was responsive to my awkward directions and never took advantage of my obvious rookie status.

I would occasionally bring the boys out to ride. Poor Speck would practically be paralyzed for fear of stepping on them. Once I had them on board, she would look at me for every move. I would lead her around the arena, first at a walk then a gentle trot (if there is such a thing). The boys loved it. Even Rich, not a natural horseman, could be persuaded to mount up and enjoy a jog around the ring.

When we were back on the ground, Speck would tenderly nuzzle us but never tried to bite, kick or do anything unladylike. Her original trainer taught her to be obedient, disciplined and considerate. They also must have worked kindly with her for she possessed a refined manner and a gentle spirit.

Sensing my initial awkwardness Speck showed her docile side with me, but as I grew more confident so did she. She never gave me more than I could handle, she waited until I was ready for the next step. I was amazed one day during a lesson when my instructor hopped on Speck. They galloped around the arena performing tight turns and quick direction changes. The moves she used to do as a barrel racer. They were both having fun. I clapped enthusiastically after this demonstration of Speck's talent. I was also humbled when I thought of how gently this rodeo queen treated me when she was capable of so much more.

I wasn't a Christian yet when Speck and I rode together but I believe God took this opportunity to teach me a heart lesson from a sensitive, spotted mare. A lesson without words (which often get in the way) of the gentleness God would soon expect from me.

Lessons from a blue ribbon winner:

1. Be aware of the person next to you and be sensitive to their needs and feelings.
2. Don't step on toes.
3. Cooperate and be helpful whenever possible.
4. Adjust yourself to the ability of others. Control your behavior even (or especially) when you have the power to act otherwise.
5. Be clear and consistent in your communication. We teach other people how to treat us.

6. Look to the one leading you (God) before taking off at a gallop.
7. Avoid electric fences at all costs. They snap and sound like a snake which may cause you to go berserk before you realize it's too late—Speck's one weakness. Sound familiar? (Genesis 3).

For the kingdom of God is not a matter of talk but of power.
What do you prefer? Shall I come to you with a whip
or in love and with a gentle spirit?
Corinthians 4:20-21

The basin and the towel. Jesus' gentle example.

My friend, Maria, and I worked together for several years. I wish I had time to tell about all the experiences we shared. I will tell you she is one of the godliest, bravest and gentlest people I know.

We worked and laughed and cried and prayed together. No matter the circumstances, Maria lived in the presence of God. He wasn't simply a special part of her life, a large piece of the pie, He *was* her life.

Maria had the same problems we all have (and maybe a few more) but she faced them with God and kept going. With clients, patients, and staff she was calm, listened carefully and responded with gentle words and a heart of love even when she needed to be firm and convey difficult information. People trusted Maria because she didn't make things complicated. She did what needed doing and said what needed saying with simplicity and gentleness.

Maria reminds me of the story of Jesus as He washed the disciple's feet at the Passover Feast. The washing should have been done by a servant but Jesus took it on Himself.

...so he got up from the meal, took off his outer clothing, and
wrapped a towel around his waist. After that, he poured water into
a basin and began to wash his disciples' feet, drying them with the
towel that was wrapped around him.
John 13:4-5

Now, Jesus was making a point here so I don't believe He yanked the men's feet up and scoured them roughly with a pumice stone chastising them for their calluses and lack of personal hygiene. No, I think He carefully placed each of His friend's feet in the basin, loosened and massaged away the dust and grime of the road, and then gently rubbed them dry with the towel. It's an incredible picture of servanthood and grace, even if the disciples didn't quite get it.

Maria got it. She understood the tender, gentle side of servanthood. Gentleness displayed in different ways to meet different needs. She lived out foot washing in a way I could see and understand—because her gentleness and grace drew me closer to God and "washed my feet" too.

Don't play the blame game. Take a turn at gentleness instead.

Sitting at my desk on a drizzly June morning I'm trying to concentrate on gentleness. I really am. It's hard to focus, though, when the world outside my window seems to have gone mad. Wars, terrorist attacks, genocide, human trafficking, school shootings, economic instability... the list is long and the evening news predominantly bad. To top it off, the political situation in our country has become a battle of words combined with crazy accusations from each side as they try to prove the other wrong. It's nuts. It's uncivilized!

The world seems to be fueled by greed, hate, lust, power, and fear. From the actions and choices of the most powerful nations and corporations to the behavior and attitudes we display toward each other in our homes, the war to be right and have our way rages on at the expense of gentleness.

✻ ✻ ✻

"Grandma, Garrison spilled his milk," Emitt yells, sending the first volley over the bow.

"He pushed me and made it spill," Garrison fires back.

"Well, your glass was too close to the edge," Emitt tosses a grenade.

"It was not and you shouldn't sit so close to me," Garrison starts to cry. A powerful weapon.

Time for Grandma to grab a couple of towels and enter the war zone. Now, I have a choice. I can choose a side and go to war for their cause or I can remain calm and neutral, give them each a towel, and while they are cleaning up gently explain the concept of an accident. The milk was not deliberately spilled.

"Garrison, you can stop crying and Emitt you can stop pointing your finger at your brother." I remain calm even as I watch the milk drip down the heat vent.

"What can we learn from this?" I ask in my best mediator voice.

Silence.

"Well, I'll tell you," I say as they slosh the milk around on the floor. "Garrison, you need to set your glass behind your plate and, Emitt, you need to keep your hands to yourself and not touch your brother while you're at the table. This accident didn't have to happen but, because of your choices, it did. Spilled milk is not worth tattling about or crying over. You're not in trouble and I'm not blaming either one of you, but you both get to clean up the mess."

Moral of the story: everything doesn't have to be someone's fault and a gentle response can calm an otherwise explosive situation. Of course, many things, globally and on the home front, are deliberate and need to be dealt with firmly and decisively. But most things are not worth going to war. The saying, "This isn't a mountain worth dying on," is worth considering before we ignore the Spirit's prompting for a gentle response and draw our weapons.

We also need to take personal responsibility for our decisions and actions rather than looking for someone or something to bear the blame when things go wrong. We have the choice to see the situation as it really is and respond with gentleness.

❊ ❊ ❊

Rich and I vacationed in Victoria last year and visited Butchart Gardens. The day was mild and sunny and the garden crowded with visitors "oohing" and "ahhing" and snapping pictures of the beautiful flowers.

We were walking behind a Japanese couple enjoying their response to the beauty around them even though we couldn't understand what they were saying.

Suddenly, the woman stopped in front of what I thought was an insignificant little pink daisy. She bent over, placed the stem between her index and middle finger and ever so gently slid her hand up the stem until the flower rested in her palm. She spoke softly to her husband and he bent over and smiled. After a moment, she slowly removed her hand releasing the bloom unharmed.

What if we could see each other as individual blooms in the garden of God's beautiful creation, delicate and worthy of our tenderness. Could we learn to enjoy our differences and not be so quick to mow each other down? Could we be taught to look at the value of each individual and respect their right to bloom and live instead of stomping through the garden demanding our own rights and blaming others when we don't get our way? In the vast complexity of God's plan, maybe not. According to His Word, there will be, "wars and rumors of wars" (Matthew 24:6) until Christ returns.

We may not be able to control the big picture, but as individuals there are constant battles we can control. Gentleness is a choice. We can:

+ Mediate rather than blame.
+ Encourage instead of criticize.
+ Seek out a common bond rather than point out differences.
+ Be tender and considerate instead of harsh and rude.
+ Seek the best for others in place of chasing after our own wants and desires.
+ Listen to someone else's opinion as an alternative to demanding "my way or the highway."
+ Get up in the morning and decide to have a good attitude instead of allowing our feelings and actions to be tossed about by the circumstances of the day.

The opportunities to choose gentleness are woven throughout our days, we simply have to look for them and respond to the Spirit's leading.

I mentioned the word civilized in the first paragraph. It's a synonym for gentleness. As the world spins beneath our feet we, as Christians, are called to stop pushing and shoving and blaming and be a civilized people for we are citizens of the Kingdom of God. I need to quit blaming the behavior of the world for my problems, keep my eyes on Jesus, let Him settle my heart and cultivate the fruit of gentleness in my soul. If I cooperate and listen to the Holy Spirit, He will harvest the fruit and give it to those who are starving for the sweet taste of gentleness in the midst of the battle.

Let your gentleness be evident to all. The Lord is near.
Philippians 4:5

Gentleness

Sharing Fruit

🍉 **Gentle now. Don't scare or threaten people.**

I am normally a cautious driver but I have the bad habit of zipping up to stop signs then quickly breaking to a stop. *I know I'm going to stop* but the poor guy driving the car on the through street doesn't. I don't know how many times I've seen terrified then angry looks as people slammed on their breaks to avoid what seemed an inevitable crash or swerved dangerously into the other lane to get out of my way. I always feel bad for doing this and vow to change my speedy ways—until I do it again. One day I'll do it to a policeman and that will be that.

On the flip side, I hate it when drivers do this to me. Catching a car in my peripheral vision charging toward a stop sign with no apparent intention of stopping, scares me and the threat of being hit broadside can send me swerving into oncoming traffic. Why can't they start slowing down when they first see the stop sign and avoid giving me palpitations?

Why indeed? If I knew the answer, I'd stop doing it myself. Okay, now I've confessed my sin, I repent and will really, really try to turn from my wicked ways.

I share this story because "scare" and "threaten" are not gentle words and they do not describe gentle behavior. I also have to admit that I often scare and threaten people when my car is parked in the garage. I suspect from time to time we all would have to plead guilty to something on the following list:

- Cold and moody behavior or stony silence can intimidate others and cause them to "walk on eggshells" around us (or avoid us completely). Rich says there are days he lives in perpetual confusion.
- Flashes of temper catch people off guard and can frighten them or provoke them to become defensive. This damages relationships and teaches people to "keep their guard up" when they see us coming.
- Sarcasm is disrespectful and can leave people feeling mocked, ridiculed or embarrassed.
- Insensitivity to the opinions or feelings of others as we demand our rights over theirs is demeaning and demoralizing.
- Arrogance and contempt for others attacks their self-worth and devalues their humanity.
- Criticism, especially in front of others, ambushes people with humiliation and shame.
- Even actions we see as silly and harmless—like jumping out from behind a door yelling, "Boo," and the many forms that can take—often startle and undo others.

I could keep this going until my thesaurus wears out. Instead, I think I will list the opposites of these behaviors which should give us a look at what gentleness is all about.

- Warm and steady behavior and no "silent treatments."
- A calm disposition with a firm control of one's temper.
- Sincere affirmation.

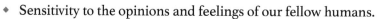
- ✦ Sensitivity to the opinions and feelings of our fellow humans.
- ✦ Humility and respectfulness.
- ✦ Praise in public and correct (not criticize) in private. Maintain a balance of truth and grace.
- ✦ Awareness of how our thoughtless actions and words affect others.

The next time you are tempted to run up to a stop sign, in word or deed, slow down and consider the consequences.

Watch the path of your feet, and all your ways will be established.
Do not turn to the right nor to the left; turn your foot from evil.
Proverbs 4:26-27 NASB

🍉 **Give gentle responses to difficult people.**

Positive responses to challenging people don't come naturally. At least not to me. I am so incredibly non-confrontational and afraid of conflict that it takes everything in me to stand my ground and respond with dignity and gentleness. The "fight or flight" response doesn't work when gentleness is needed. Other people are more confrontational by nature and face their own challenges to be gentle. Whatever our temperament, as Christians, God calls us to be like Him, "...gentle and humble in heart..." (Matthew 11:29).

In our homes, with friends, at our jobs, on the phone or in our texts and e-mails, wherever each day takes us, we face the decision to give a gentle response to hurting or difficult people. Sometimes we are the wounded or tired or cranky person and a gentle word from an open heart is balm to our soul.

I've seen gentleness calm and sooth too many situations that would have been stirred up by harsh words to question Proverbs 15:1 "A gentle answer turns away wrath, but a harsh word stirs up anger."

※ ※ ※

I've already written about Jenny, Dad's urology nurse, and her firm, calming effect on my father. She was a wonder! But she wasn't the only one.

The tube inserted through Dad's abdomen had to be removed and cleaned once a month.

This required a trip to the Urology Department of the hospital. When we arrived for the current appointment we were informed Jenny was out sick and Dad would be seeing a different nurse. Well, no he wouldn't. He became very upset and we went home.

Jenny called the next day and talked to Dad. She apologized for not being there and commiserated with him about how hard it was on him to make that trip to the hospital. She suggested a visiting health nurse come to the house, just this one time, so he could get the catheter cleaned right away. Dad agreed. Only Jenny could have convinced him of this alternate plan.

The nurse was scheduled to come the next day. Dad, of course, had a change of heart later that afternoon and wanted to cancel.

"Dad, Jenny thinks this is a good idea so let's try it out for this month," I said *nicely* (not what I was feeling) with a silent prayer that he would agree. He did.

The nurse, a man in his mid-forties and completely bald, showed up right on time the next day. He introduced himself as John and then turned to my Dad.

"You must be Mr. Smith. I'm sorry you couldn't get in to see Jenny but she said to say, "Hi," and she'll see you next month. She told me all about the tomatoes you brought her."

"Yep. Had a good crop of Early Girls this year. You have a garden?" Dad asked.

"I usually do, but I'm having chemotherapy treatments right now so don't have the energy to garden," John answered smiling and rubbing his bald head. "Next year I should feel up to it and I'll remember those Early Girls. I haven't tried that variety."

Ever subtle, Dad asked, "Well, what kind of cancer have you got?" as John followed him into the bedroom, gently holding Dad's elbow to steady him.

I didn't hear the rest of the conversation but was amazed at Dad's reaction. The procedure took only a few minutes but they continued to chat for quite a while when they came back in the living room.

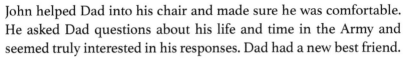

John helped Dad into his chair and made sure he was comfortable. He asked Dad questions about his life and time in the Army and seemed truly interested in his responses. Dad had a new best friend.

"John is a nice guy," Dad said after he left. "I hope he beats that cancer. Maybe he can come again next month so I don't have to go up to that #%*&# hospital. I would miss Jenny but it's sure easier to have the blasted thing changed here."

Dad didn't have to have the catheter changed again. He died three weeks later. I am very grateful for John. He treated a cranky, frightened, dying man with gentleness and respect. They talked and even laughed together. He acknowledged my father's humanity and blessed him with his own.

I think I caught a glimpse of Jesus in John that day. I sure hope he beat that cancer.

> *Congenial conversation—what a pleasure!*
> *The right word at the right time—beautiful!*
> Proverbs 15:23 MSG

🍉 **Gently soften awkward or embarrassing moments.**

As the guest speaker at a small church, I waited in the second row for the pastor's introduction. When he called my name and motioned for me to come forward, I stood up and headed toward the three steps leading to the platform. On the second step, I walked out of my right shoe which tumbled back down into the aisle.

I couldn't ignore it so had to walk back down and slip it on. The church was silent. When I successfully scaled the stairs, the pastor smiled, patted my shoulder and smiling said,

"Great attention getter."

"Works every time," I said smiling back. The congregation laughed and so did I. The quick-thinking pastor turned an embarrassing moment into a great ice-breaker.

He demonstrated to me and his church how to be a real *gentle*man.

❊ ❊ ❊

Here's another one—I could tell these all day.

Recently promoted from a teller position to the trust department of the bank where I worked, I attended a luncheon in a very prestigious downtown club surrounded by a table full of bank officers in suits. I was a nervous wreck.

I did fine until I reached for the white carafe for a refill of coffee. I unscrewed the lid and tipped the pot over my cup—sending hot coffee splashing all over the table in front of me. I was mortified. Apparently there was a trick button to push before pouring.

Before the last drop landed, though, a waiter stepped calmly up to the table with a fluffy, white towel in hand. Sliding in next to me he began mopping up coffee until the cloth was a sodden, brown mass.

"I'm so sorry, Miss. Are you all right? I must have left the lid loose when I refilled the pot. I apologize for my carelessness and for ruining your meal. I'll be right back with a fresh sandwich and cup of coffee." He backed through a door behind me before I could think of anything to say.

No one at the table seemed particularly concerned. Fortunately the coffee hadn't splashed on any of those suits. The waiter returned with a new meal and fresh coffee.

"There you go, Miss. Again, I'm so sorry for your inconvenience." He gave me a gentle smile as he turned away.

All I wanted to do was go home and have a good cry but this dear man had thrown himself into the breach and taken the blame for my blunder. I looked for him as we left the dining room hoping to have a chance to say, "thank you," but couldn't find him. Then, I saw him holding the front door open for the group as they filed out onto the street. As I walked in front of him I caught his eye and said, "Thank you so much."

He simply grinned and said, "My pleasure, Miss."

It was another ten years before I accepted Christ as my Savior but I believe He was already teaching me the power of gentleness to come to the aid of someone in distress.

Be completely humble and gentle; be patient,
bearing with one another in love.
Ephesians 4:2

Gentle strength.

Our daughter-in-law went into serious labor on a November afternoon and we were called to come stay with Ranger our grand-dog as he suffered from separation anxiety. The three of us slept in the same bed. Ranger slept great but Rich and I were bleary-eyed when the phone rang the next morning and Matt informed us that Emitt had finally arrived by C-section. We threw ourselves together, fed the dog, and headed for the hospital.

Matt met us in the hall and told us about the importance of thorough hand washing and *no* coughing or sneezing. We had just slept with a shedding black Lab and had not had time to shower but we kept our mouths shut and did what we were told. We wanted to get our hands on that baby!

Once we were cleared for entrance we stopped and paid homage to dear Michele who produced this little miracle for us. Then, like magnets, we were drawn to the bassinet. We instantly fell in love with this tiny bundle and, of course, my instinct was to reach down, pick up this new person and introduce myself. Matthew, however was right behind me and told me to sit down and he would hand Emitt to me. I smiled and sat.

Tears welled in my eyes as I watched my big, strong, grown-up son gently lift his baby and snuggle him to his chest. He explained how to hold Emitt, support his head and properly swaddle him after I had checked his fingers and toes. Rich stood behind me, waiting his turn, as Matt hovered and told us all about labor and delivery. Occasionally he would walk over to the bed and touch Michele's face as she dozed.

I watched as Matt stepped into his new role of father without missing a beat. I was overwhelmed with our new little grandson but also by seeing a side of my son I didn't know existed. Gentleness, tenderness and a confidence I hadn't expected brought tears to my eyes.

He is still capable of great tenderness toward his boys even though the second one, Garrison, was handed off in the hospital like a football. No instructions needed.

Strength coupled with gentleness. Sounds familiar.

Let the little children come to me,
and do not hinder them for the kingdom of God belongs to
such as these...And he took the children in his arms,
put his hands on them and blessed them.
Mark 10:14-16

I believe this is how we are to treat all God's children, not just the little ones.

 **Burden Bearers.**

"Thud."

Something hit the sliding glass doors in the family room. My ten-year-old son, James, and I were on our feet to see what caused the noise. We were stopped by the sight of a good sized bird lying motionless next to the door.

"He must have hit the door," I said. "Go out and see if he's breathing."

"Why me?" James asked. "What if he's dead?"

"Just do it," I said feeling guilty because I was afraid. "I'll call the Audubon Society and ask what we should do if he's alive."

The lady at the Audubon Society was very helpful and told us to gently put him in a shoebox with a lid and place him in a cool, safe place for two hours. At the end of two hours, tap the box and if there's movement, take it outside and remove the lid. If the bird's collision with the door stunned him and he wasn't injured, he should fly away. She became slightly cool when I told her we had four cats. I promised to bring them all in before releasing the bird (unless, of course, it was dead).

"He's breathing," James reported when I got off the phone. I went looking for a shoebox and told him to watch for cats.

I returned with a box lined with a small towel and poked with air holes. James, ever so gently, picked up the still unconscious bird and placed him in the box, telling him not to worry he would be okay. He bonded easily. We closed the lid, took the box out to the garage (no cats) and put a book on the lid in case he woke up and tried to escape. Then we rounded up the cats and waited.

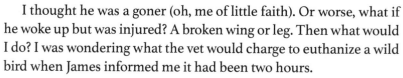

I thought he was a goner (oh, me of little faith). Or worse, what if he woke up but was injured? A broken wing or leg. Then what would I do? I was wondering what the vet would charge to euthanize a wild bird when James informed me it had been two hours.

We tip-toed out to the garage and gently tapped the box.

"Flutter, scratch, cheeeeep," was the response.

We removed the book but held the lid firmly as birdie was now quite active. All I needed was a bird loose in the house with four cats. I knew somehow the Audubon lady would find out.

We carried the box close to the trees and slowly lifted the lid. The bird poked his head out, looked around (probably checking for more invisible walls), gave himself a shake and after a short rest in our maple tree, flew away.

We were both a little shaky so went for ice cream.

As we lapped at our mint chocolate chip ice cream cones, I thought about all the people who are living life, minding their own business, when they run into a wall they didn't see coming. Thud! Something outside the realm of daily life. The death of someone close, loss of a job, a serious diagnosis, an unfaithful spouse, a natural disaster, a car crash, a house fire...there are so many unexpected physical and emotional events that can knock us for a loop and leave us stunned. Still breathing but not functioning very well.

These people (possibly you or me) need someone to come alongside and do whatever practical things need doing. Then we need to stay nearby and wait. As much as we are allowed, we need to speak softly, stay close and provide physical and emotional safety. With permission, a gentle hug or touch on the shoulder can calm and reassure—there is comfort in human contact. And prayer—lots of prayer.

Of course, our own lives resume and need to be lived, but we need to maintain close contact as much as possible. Weave these hurting people into our lives. There are no guarantees that their life will return to normal. We all hit walls and "normal" tends to change from time to time, but we are to be a gentle whisper of hope in their darkness until the light begins to shine again. When they are ready, take them for ice cream.

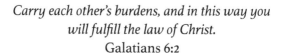

Carry each other's burdens, and in this way you
will fulfill the law of Christ.
Galatians 6:2

FRUIT FOR THOUGHT

Gentleness

Nurturing Fruit

1. Is it easy or difficult for you to accept God's gentleness and trust you are safe in His arms—regardless of your circumstances (that's the catch!)?

2. Do you agree we are all fragile regardless of our outward appearance? Are you able to respond with gentleness toward difficult people even if your feelings are hurt or you are provoked? (This is hard to do so you will need to practice and pray for a gentle mindset).

3. Re-read "Lessons from a blue ribbon winner" in "Horse Sense" and write a brief statement addressing an area where change may be needed in your life. What's your "electric fence?"

4. Who needs a gentle "foot washing" in your life?

5. Have you ever blamed someone (or something) else for a consequence of your actions? Have you ever had it done to you? What did it accomplish? What difference would a gentle response have made?

Sharing Fruit

1. Have you been guilty of any of the behaviors in the first list under "Don't scare or threaten people?" What gentle qualities from the second list would you like to adapt into your own life and share with others?

2. How do you normally respond to difficult people? If you tend to be a bit snippy, how could you gentle your reaction? Anything you would need to overcome? What behaviors would be helpful when facing a challenging individual?

3. Have you been in an awkward or embarrassing situation and been rescued by a gentle soul? Is there a time when you intervened for someone in distress?

4. Have you experienced or witnessed strength coupled with gentleness? What did that look like and how did you feel? In what areas of your life are you called to be strong and gentle at the same time?

5. Have you or has someone close to you run into an "invisible wall?" Did someone come alongside? Describe the situation. Have you come alongside someone stunned by something they didn't see coming? What was their reaction? How can you cultivate a heart that is gentle, sensitive and responsive to this kind of need?

Grab your notebook and write out...

◆ One Scripture from this chapter that is particularly meaningful to you.

◆ Your Thoughts and Stories

Chapter Nine

THE FRUIT OF THE SPIRIT IS ... SELF-CONTROL

Quiet Please!

"Why do you usually wait before giving your opinion at staff meetings?" I asked my boss, Julie.

She thought for a moment before answering (of course). "I want to make sure I say what I really think and that it will be helpful to the discussion."

What a novel idea. I tend to be a verbal processor. You've heard the saying, "I don't know what I think until I say it." That's me. At least it used to be. Flinging words out into the fresh air and then deciding if I really believe them is a risky way to live. It's a great quality for "think-tank" sessions where anything goes. In general conversation it can leave you looking foolish (at best) and cause a lot of backtracking, crow eating and apologizing.

I began observing people who overcame the urge to insert a comment into every available bit of air space. They invariably appeared smarter than me. I found a plaque that said, "The Best Substitute for Brains Is Silence" and put it over my stove. It's taken a while to sink in—probably because I don't spend much time cooking—but I'm starting to get it.

Growing up an only child I was extremely shy and rarely spoke up or offered an opinion. I never raised my hand in class. Then in my early thirties, right after I became a Christian, a spiritual and verbal metamorphosis took place. The accumulation of unused words just started pouring out. Unfortunately, listening to the Spirit came a bit later.

In my enthusiasm, I offered opinions where they weren't needed, interrupted and finished people's sentences and gave out way more information than necessary. It was kind of scary.

At the same time I ceased really listening to what others had to say. Instead, I waited for them to be quiet so I could talk. I often hurt or offended people or came across as insensitive. I simply didn't think through the consequences of my words.

People like that annoy me. Gradually it began to register. The people I admired, respected and viewed as role models were the ones who listened well and kept their mouths shut more than open.

The sound of my own voice began to wear on my nerves so I decided to give it a rest. Habits are hard to break but I'm finally finding a middle ground between the silence of my childhood and the "Chatty Annie" of my middle years. I still love spontaneous conversation with safe people who love you no matter what—it's fun—but, even then, I'm learning to be careful.

The habit of allowing my words and actions to run ahead of my brain has been a major cause of grief and embarrassment in my adult life. God has a lot to say on this subject in His Word. The more I study and learn His will for me in this area, the more I pay attention when the Holy Spirit warns me to put the brakes on.

Here are a few Scriptures that helped a reforming talkaholic:

When words are many, sin is not absent,
but he who holds his tongue is wise.
Proverbs 10:19

A fool finds no pleasure in understanding
but delights in airing his own opinions.
Proverbs 18:2

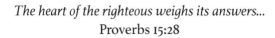

The heart of the righteous weighs its answers...
Proverbs 15:28

There are untold numbers of ways we can lack self-control in our lives. This is only *one* of mine. Self-control is a choice and it's amazing how often we choose wrong. If this were a test, the answer key is God's Word and the power to make the right choice is the Holy Spirit. I can muster up all manner of good intentions but I must first surrender my self-will to the Spirit of God for there to be any control.

Lack of self-control probably attracts more spiritual fruit flies than anything else. Just as love is the foundation of the Fruit of the Spirit, lack of self-control can often be the wrecking ball. When we choose self-control, we choose to uphold God's foundation of love.

Most of us occasionally struggle with submitting our will to the control of the Holy Spirit and mess up. If the story ended there, why bother trying—but it doesn't. God loves us and knows our willy-nilly ways. He sent Jesus for us. We can take our spiritual fruit flies to Him, ask for His help and forgiveness and, by the power of the Spirit walk into a new day with a basket of fresh fruit and a fresh start. God wants us to be His fruit-bearers to the world. He will give us the power and grace to overcome ourselves.

Self-Control

Nurturing Fruit

 Read a chapter from Proverbs every day.

My friend (and boss), Julie, introduced me to this practice. It took a bit of self-control to get going but soon I was hooked. This plan works great as there are thirty-one chapters in Proverbs. On the months with thirty days, I still read chapter thirty-one.

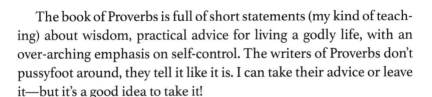

The book of Proverbs is full of short statements (my kind of teaching) about wisdom, practical advice for living a godly life, with an over-arching emphasis on self-control. The writers of Proverbs don't pussyfoot around, they tell it like it is. I can take their advice or leave it—but it's a good idea to take it!

Try reading different Bible translations and paraphrases. If God doesn't get His point across in one, He will in another.

As you already know, my wayward words tend to be a problem. This issue is addressed frequently in Proverbs. Reading different Bible versions helps embed the idea or command a little deeper in my forgetful brain. Here are good examples from Proverbs 10:19:

The more talk, the less truth; the wise measure their words (MSG)

Don't talk so much. You keep putting your foot in your mouth.
Be sensible and turn off the flow! (TLB) I sure heard this one!

On the introduction page to the Book of Proverbs in my Bible (NASB) I have written, "Proverbs teach us to *choose* to *act* in accord with the mind and heart of God." Although the words remain the same, my life is in a different place every time I read through the book. God never fails to speak to my current situation, thoughts or behavior and help me choose to act according to His will. I will always be grateful to Julie for encouraging me in this spiritual discipline.

A friend loves at all times...
Proverbs 17:17

Listen to advice and accept instruction, and in the end you will be wise.
Proverbs 19:20

 Get a grip on your thought life.

My thoughts are currently following my eyes as I watch the squirrels from an upstairs window. The canopy of trees in our backyard provides an excellent playground for these nutty critters. Two of them are chasing each other from branch to branch, tree to tree. They have no plan, just enthusiasm and seemingly boundless energy.

We've shared our yard with squirrels for over forty years and I've always enjoyed their goofy ways. They can outsmart any birdfeeder (especially the ones designed to keep out squirrels), their aerial acrobatics are amazing and they can keep the cats entertained until catnap time.

However, someone in our neighborhood gives them peanuts (not me!) which they bury all over our yard. Rich doesn't see the humor in this and tends to agree with Sarah Jessica Parker's comment, "Squirrels are just rats with cuter outfits."

These little rodents (depending on whose side you're on) tend to get themselves into trouble. They like to tease our cats and the neighbor's dog by running around on the ground and then racing up the nearest tree. Occasionally, though, they get so focused digging up the flower beds trying to remember where they hid the peanuts they forget there are felines prowling around. Sometimes they get caught!

They also like to play the squirrel version of "chicken" racing back and forth across the street, often stopping in the middle of the road for no apparent reason. Sometimes they get squished.

I won't give the details of what happens when they go exploring inside electrical transformers except to say there is a neighborhood power outage and a fried squirrel.

As I watch these nut-jobs, I begin to realize how similar my thoughts and actions are to their behavior and occasional consequences. If I'm not focused on something, my thoughts often bounce around looking for somewhere to land. Sometimes they land safely where God would like them to be and sometimes they fly off following temptations and trouble. Either way, my thoughts—good or bad—can turn into actions. Like the squirrels, I've found myself caught, squished or fried. Not good. I need to remember and heed what Paul said in 2 Corinthians 10:5:

We demolish arguments and every pretension that sets itself up against the knowledge of God, and we take captive every thought to make it obedient to Christ.

So, I'm learning to nurture my good thoughts and ask God to help me jettison the negative or crummy ones before they put down roots and grow into a tree I can't get out of.

Where do my thoughts go when I'm not paying attention? If they're grumbling, or stewing or plotting revenge, I need to deal with them swiftly. The most difficult thoughts to get rid of are the ones I enjoy (like self-pity). Similar to wiggling a loose tooth, they hurt and feel good at the same time. Faced with these mental troublemakers, it's a good idea to remember that a cute squirrel can be a sneaky rat in disguise. I've used this verse before but it applies here so I'll use it again in a different version.

Finally, brethren, whatever is true, whatever is honorable, whatever is
right, whatever is pure, whatever is lovely, whatever is of good repute,
if there is any excellence and if anything worthy of praise,
let your mind dwell on these things.
Philippians 4:8 NASB

 Do all things in moderation—unless you shouldn't be doing them at all!

Moderation and self-control are not virtues highly prized in our culture. We can't be too thin or too rich. We have oversized houses, TVs and SUVs. Magazines, television, all forms of advertising immerse us in the deep water of wants and perceived needs. Prescription meds, alcohol, sex, food, power, any and all indulgences are prescribed by the world to make us happy. Being "medium" is hard. Living "simply" is a difficult challenge. Tranquility is illusive. Moderation is not an easy choice. Sometimes we are so overloaded we begin to unravel and sometimes come undone.

Ask for help if you need to. Weight (our female common denominator), addictions, depression and anger are just a few of the issues often too difficult to conquer on our own. Ask God for guidance and your doctor for his help and good referrals if needed. I have been part of a support group and was blessed and greatly helped by the strength and compassion I found through others dealing with an issue similar to mine. I've also seen a wonderful therapist who helped me see my life and perceived problems through a different set of eyes—very helpful.

Most of my struggles with moderation and self-control are of the selfish variety.

- What's wrong with spending $120 every eight weeks to have my hair cut and colored? (I think I just heard my husband choke!)
- I'll never be happy until I can wear a size four (like that will ever happen!) Those of you who wear itty, bitty sizes probably have something else that niggles at you.
- If I have to live in this 1970's house with popcorn ceilings for the rest of my life, I'll scream.
- I deserve better than this (whatever "this" is for you). Do I? Do you?

I recently read a sign (at Fabric Land of all places) that said, "There are many people in this world who are very happy with far less than what you have." I stopped. I put back the goofy yard ornament I had in my hand.

Is my striving and longing for more and better causing a discontented and unsettled heart? Am I relying on the accumulation of things and experiences to replace the promises of God? Why, yes, I believe I am. I believe my unwillingness to settle down and accept the blessings and freedom that come with moderation disguise my faith.

This doesn't apply to everyone but I think many American Christians, including me, are often more enmeshed with the culture than with Christ. Our heads have been turned. It takes self-control to turn back and live Christ-centered lives.

I'm not trying to take us on a guilt trip. We don't need to don sackcloth and ashes and have really bad hair. We don't need to erase all images of our dream house or vacation. We simply need to turn our eyes from the things of the world to the eyes of Jesus. He knows what we need and what we want and He loves us.

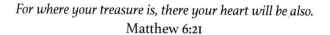

For where your treasure is, there your heart will be also.
Matthew 6:21

But seek first His kingdom and His righteousness;
and all these things shall be added unto you.
Matthew 6:33 NASB

Beware of losing control in the "impact zone."

On vacation in Kona on the big island of Hawaii, Rich and I walked an uneven path of lava and white coral along the edge of the Pacific. The view encompassed so much beauty our eyes couldn't hold it all. There isn't much beach as the lava runs out to the sea and the surf crashes into the rocks sending hair frizzing spray into the air.

A young Hawaiian man walked toward us with his surf board under his arm. We shared "Alohas" and stepped aside to let him pass. Just before he got away from me I blurted out, "How do you keep from crashing into the jagged lava? It looks so dangerous."

He stopped and smiled, probably accustomed to questions from ghostly white or painfully sunburned tourists.

"It is dangerous." He answered. "I've been surfing here since I was eight or so and the ocean still fools me sometimes. The trick is to avoid the impact zone."

I looked confused so he continued.

"I look for a smooth patch of water, paddle out and wait for a good wave. I ride until I feel the subtle pull of the current then turn aside while I still have control of the board. If I wait too long the waves will take over my speed and direction, catch me up and toss me onto the lava. You really don't want that to happen." He showed us scars on his legs and one arm.

I was just about to ask why on earth he even stuck a toe in the water but I think he could sense my next question and turned back to the path.

"Aloha. Have a good day," he said as he walked away.

"Aloha," we called back.

When I was sure he couldn't hear me I turned to Rich and said, "Nutso."

Rich smiled. He knows I tend to transfer my fear of water onto everyone else. It truly amazes me what some people do for fun, but that's not what this story is about.

The phrase, "avoid the impact zone" stuck in my head.

How many times have I failed to quit talking when I should and crashed into verbal rocks? I've over-eaten and gone to bed with waves of heartburn no amount of Tums could sooth. I've used my credit card to purchase "wants" when I knew I didn't have enough money. I hit the jagged lava when the bill arrived. You get the picture.

I can live and work and play contentedly in the safety of the bounty and beauty God has provided. Or, I can go for one more "last word," one more bite, one more toy, and crash. Out of control, I allow my greed or gluttony or lust (an icky but accurate word) or simply carelessness to sweep me out of safe waters where the waves take over.

Remember the surfer's words, "look for the smooth water" and "avoid the impact zone." Remember David's words in Psalm 23:2-3, "...he leads me beside quiet waters, he restores my soul. He guides me in paths of righteousness for his name's sake..." Be aware of your particular waves of temptation and ask God to help you turn away before you're swept away.

No temptation has seized you except what is common to man.
And God is faithful; he will not let you be tempted beyond what you can
bear. But when you are tempted, he will also provide a way out so that
you can stand up under it.
1 Corinthians 10:13

 Get dressed. Self-control is always fashionable.

Many women I know look coordinated and accessorized even for a trip to the grocery store. They always look put-together. Make-up, jewelry— even with a simple pair of jeans they look great. This flair for fashion seems to come naturally.

I get dressed. I've worn the same brand of make-up since high school, don the same earrings every day and keep my wardrobe very simple. I'm not saying I'm a total slob, but I have learned over the years that, for me, simplicity works best. Sometimes I stare into the closet (similar to standing in front of the open refrigerator) looking for something different (aka. fashionable) to appear but, unless someone goes shopping for me, that's probably not going to happen.

Anyway, regardless of how I dress and the accessories I choose, there is one crucial garment I need to put on every day. The armor of God. I never go outside without clothing and make-up but I frequently wander out into the world without putting on the protection God has provided for me.

Satan knows my weak spots and if I'm unprotected the battle can be over before I know what hit me. When I worked in ministry we prayed at the beginning of each shift. My supervisor would often have us stand up and pretend to put on the armor of God as she read Ephesians 6:10-17. She knew the enemy didn't want us to be effective in our work and that our only defense was a good offense, God's armor.

Finally, be strong in the Lord and in His mighty power.
Put on the full armor of God so that you can take your stand against
the devil's schemes. For our struggle is not against flesh and blood,
but against the rulers, against the authorities, against the powers
of this dark world and against the spiritual forces of evil in the
heavenly realms. Therefore put on the full armor of God, so that
when the day of evil comes, you may be able to stand your ground,
and after you have done everything, to stand. Stand firm then,
with the belt of truth buckled around your waist, with the breastplate
of righteousness in place, and with your feet fitted with the readiness
that comes from the gospel of peace. In addition to all this, take
up the shield of faith, with which you can extinguish all the flaming
arrows of the evil one. Take the helmet of salvation and the sword
of the Spirit, which is the word of God.

This incredible outfit of security and strength hangs in all our closets. Regardless of our individual style of dress, the armor goes with everything.

Self-control in this world can be pretty tricky on our own but with our armor on we can say with Paul,

I can do all things through him who gives me strength.
Philippians 4:13

Self-Control

Sharing Fruit

 Install a self-control filter...available through the Holy Spirit.

As I changed the filter on the kitchen tap the other day I realized that's what I need—a filter between my head and my mouth. A Holy Spirit filter. There is a space between stimulus and reaction where I *choose* my response. A space available to stop, think and pray. A pause to monitor my inner voice and focus my thinking. This doesn't have to take forever, just a couple of heartbeats for the Holy Spirit to edit my speech. If I'm paying any attention at all, He will make it very clear what should and shouldn't come out my mouth. Sometimes I'm still overcome with the urge to talk and ignore His warnings. I always regret it. When I listen and hold my tongue I'm amazed at how much I learn and how easily the conversation manages to get along without my constant input. Ask God to install a self-control filter between your brain, your mouth and your actions. Be aware of that space and pray for sensitivity and obedience to the Spirit's prompting (if you ask, He *will* prompt!)

Set a guard, O LORD, over my mouth; keep watch over
the door of my lips.
Psalm 141:3 (NASB)

Our family recently embarked on the adventure of juicing. This entails the purchase and cleaning of vast quantities of fruits and vegetables (organic, of course) and shoving them down the tube of a very large, expensive machine. The juice empties into a pitcher on one side and the pulp fills a bag in the container on the other side. The idea is that you could never eat enough fruit and veggies to get all the nutritional goodies you gulp down in a glass of juice.

You may be wondering where I'm going with this story. I'm sort of wondering myself but I think I've got it. What if I take all the thoughts and feelings, moods and prejudices, whatever is rattling around the hallways of my head and heart and ask the Holy Spirit to forgive the sinful stuff and use the good stuff? He'll put it all into His version of a juicer and turn it on. As all my raw material hits the filter the good stuff will come out (in my speech, attitude, actions and body language) and the inappropriate gunk will get tossed.

The catch is I have to be plugged into the Spirit and remember to ask Him to turn on the filter. This is hard at first. I like to talk. Spill everything out and clean up the mess later. God apparently is tired of my messes. He is teaching me to let the Spirit operate His "juicer." If I choose obedience, I find my thoughts, words, attitude and actions are sweeter and my soul healthier. The disposal of the gunk (sin) frees me and lightens my heart.

My husband wants me to add that there are all sorts of healthy recipes for the pulp (also, muffins and other fattening goodies) or, it could be composted. I told him this did not fit with my analogy but he thought you should know.

So, install that filter right away. The Holy Spirit will instruct you (though some self-control is required). Now, turn it on. The Spirit will help you think healthier thoughts, speak fewer and choicer words, and act in a manner that honors God.

And it won't cost $159.99 and leave you feeling guilty when you throw out the pulp. Sorry, Rich.

...be renewed in the spirit of your mind...
Ephesians 4:23 NASB

*Do not let any unwholesome talk come out of your mouths,
but only what is helpful for building others up according to their needs,
that it may benefit those who listen.*
Ephesians 4:29

🍍 **Control yourself. Don't create problems.**

I love to read newspaper interviews of elderly couples who have been married for sixty-plus years. They are always entertaining, especially when the wife gets a little snippy with her husband or the husband corrects the wife's version of a story. But every now and again one of the two casually passes along a jewel of wisdom. Here is one God used to change my life:

"Gerald, what would you say is the reason your marriage has lasted so long?" the reporter asked the husband.

"Well, young man, if I don't create a problem I don't have to fix one. It's worked well for me," the eighty-seven year old man answered. I'm sure he chuckled when he said it.

His wife, Margie's, answer to the same question almost made me fall out of my chair laughing.

"Neither one of us has died," she said. I hope *she* was chuckling.

Great reading.

It was Gerald's response, though, that got me thinking. "If I don't create a problem I don't have to fix one." I am a problem creator. I'm good at it. I've had lots of years to practice. I've also spent a lot of time doing repair work on strained relationships.

"Rich, that laurel hedge needs trimming. It's too tall and I think it has bugs on it."

"Yep, I think you're right."

"Well, we can't afford to hire someone to trim it and I think we need to get a special ladder. We'll have to borrow a truck or rent one to haul it all away." I continued to build my case.

Now, at this point you need to know two things.

1. The hedge has been too tall and buggy for at least four years and no one cared.
2. When I use the pronoun "we" when talking to Rich about projects, I really mean "you."

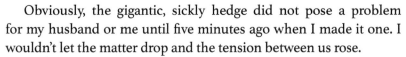

Obviously, the gigantic, sickly hedge did not pose a problem for my husband or me until five minutes ago when I made it one. I wouldn't let the matter drop and the tension between us rose.

Last weekend Rich went out and cut the hedge off at the ground. Problem solved.

The more I think about this I realize I can create problems out of thin air and work myself into a tizzy, then expect someone else to fix it. I can take a pleasant Sunday afternoon and turn it into a tense evening full of resentment and unrealistic expectations. As I look back over the years, I can see myself lighting one little, initially insignificant, fire after another. Like a problem pyromaniac. How could this be a revelation to me after all these years?

Here I am writing about living out the Fruit of the Spirit and I'm handing out sour apples at home. Once again, God is pointing out the main reason I'm writing this book. He wants me to examine my own life and heart. Am I willing to humble my rebellious self before God and submit to his teaching? Will I let Him influence my actions, my decisions, the thoughts in my brain and the words that come out of my mouth?

My answer is, "YES!" I don't want to be like the contentious wife who is a "constant dripping" in Proverbs 19:13. God is going to really have to help me here as I don't know a thing about plumbing and the faucet is still dripping. I long to be "...like a tree firmly planted by streams of water, which yields its fruit in season and whose leaf does not wither..." (Psalm 1:3).

Thank You, Lord, for all the inventive ways you use to get your message through to me. I want to honor You and recognize the value and dignity of everyone you place in my life. Help me follow the guidelines for self-control in Your Word and overcome the bad habit of creating problems just because I can. And thank you for Gerald.

Better a dry crust with peace and quiet than a house
full of feasting, with strife.
Proverbs 17:1

It is to a man's honor to avoid strife...
Proverbs 20:3

Starting a quarrel is like breaching a dam;
so drop the matter before a dispute breaks out.
Proverbs 17:14

Is someone tripping over me? Is self-control needed?

Early in my walk with Jesus I attended a prayer meeting at a local church. I gobbled up the teaching like a starving kitten. Later we divided into groups for prayer. This was new to me but I was game. I prayed out loud for the first time. My words were awkward but genuine.

After we had all lifted our prayers to the Lord, one of the women said she would like to pray specifically for each one in the group. I felt a bit nervous but hung in there.

She went around the circle, placed her hand on each person's head, and prayed a special Scripture over them. Until she came to me. Her hand firmly on my head, she said, "I don't have a Scripture for you. There are big blocks inside you and I can't see past them."

I was embarrassed but, worse than that, I felt there was something wrong with me. Maybe I wasn't a Christian at all. Maybe I didn't belong there.

I know this woman meant well but she single-handedly created a big stumbling block to my faith and growth as a believer. Looking back, I can imagine Jesus cringing at her words.

I spent a long time trying to figure out what the "blocks" represented. I knew there was still sin in my life and I had issues from my past to work on but I thought Jesus covered all that on the cross. I thought He would continue to help and heal me. Was I wrong?

I finally shared the experience and my feelings with a mature Christian friend.

"Oh, for Heaven's sake," she said, shaking her head. "I'm afraid you were shot by friendly fire."

"Huh?" was my intelligent response.

"I'm sure the woman meant you no harm," she said, touching

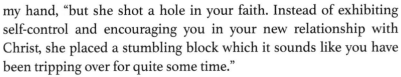

my hand, "but she shot a hole in your faith. Instead of exhibiting self-control and encouraging you in your new relationship with Christ, she placed a stumbling block which it sounds like you have been tripping over for quite some time."

"In Romans 14:13," she continued, Paul says, "Therefore let us stop passing judgment on one another. Instead, make up your mind not to put any stumbling block or obstacle in your brother's way." She then went on to pray, asking God to remove this "rock of stumbling" from my mind and heart and clear the way for the Holy Spirit to move freely through my life.

Wow. What a relief.

Obviously this made an impression on my newborn Christian psyche but God used the experience to impress on me the importance of not being a stumbling block to others. There are so many ways we can cause others to stumble I can't begin to know or list them all.

However, I do know we are to attempt to respect and understand each other. We don't need to squabble over denominational differences if salvation through faith in Christ is a common denominator.

We are all at different places in our journey with Christ so we are not to be judgmental or critical if people aren't at the same place we are.

We have great freedom in Christ but if that freedom impinges on another's beliefs, muster up self-control and don't go there.

We are individuals but we live in community with fellow believers and non-believers. We are personally responsible to be aware of the people around us and to choose to behave appropriately in every situation. This isn't easy with all the temptation the world throws at us so pray God will keep you from being a rock in someone's road.

One of the most convicting verses on this subject is Matthew 18:6, "But if anyone causes one of these little ones who believe in me to sin, it would be better for him to have a large millstone hung around his neck and to be drowned in the depths of the sea." Not good!

Our behavior makes an impression on every life we touch. We certainly don't want people to see us as phony and self-righteous. You know, the Pharisee type. With the help of the Holy Spirit and a healthy dose of self-control, we want them to see real women who love God and people, and are trying to live out the Fruit of the Spirit. I'm sure old habits will trip us up from time to time but we can trust God to protect those around us and to help us grow fruit not stumbling blocks.

Rich wanted me to share a story here.

When he was a boy he attended a church close to their house. He won a new Bible for perfect attendance. He was so excited he went across the street to show his neighbor who was deeply religious and a Grandfather figure to Rich.

"Look at my new Bible," he said, holding it up proudly.

The neighbor took the Bible, looked inside, and handed it back. "That Bible's no good, it's not King James," he said gruffly. End of discussion. End of Rich's joy over his Bible. This little boy I later married put away the Bible feeling ashamed. He quit going to church.

He turned back to God and became a Christian at age forty-three. All those years feeling separate from God because one old man's pious comment and lack of self-control belittled his Bible and fledgling faith.

He now possesses a well-worn, well-read NIV Bible. So there!

Let us therefore make every effort to do what leads to peace and to mutual edification.
Romans 14:19

Accept one another, then, just as Christ accepted you, in order to bring praise to God.
Romans 15:7

Stand firm.

Rich and I took our grandsons to see Pete's Dragon last week. We were all touched by the love and mutual caring between Pete and Elliott (the dragon). Pete had lost his parents and Elliott had become separated from his family. During the six years they lived together in the forest, Elliott displayed very un-dragon like behavior. In fact, he expressed love, joy, peace, patience, kindness, goodness, faithfulness, gentleness and (up until the end) self-control.

I don't want to spoil the movie for you but, although Elliott did use a small puff of fire to start campfires, we didn't know Elliott could breathe big dragon fire until he and the boy he loved were threatened. Now, the analogy breaks down here a bit as Elliott would have torched everyone if Pete hadn't calmed him down. Self-control really isn't a dragon's strong suit. But Elliott grabbed my heart when, weak and frightened he rose up in all his winged, green-dragon power and glory and took a stand for what mattered. He breathed fire.

I cried.

I'm not advocating we go around breathing fire or being wacky zealots but I do believe God intends us to take a stand. Somewhere, for something. After all, He gave us armor so He must foresee battles to be fought and stands to be taken.

For many years God recruited me to stand for women, children and families. Then He raised up others to fight in that arena and moved my battle to the home front. Caring for aging parents, walking through cancer with my daughter-in-law and difficulties with my precious grown sons required keeping my armor on and oiled. Now God has "set my feet in a spacious place," (Psalm 31:8) to stand for my husband, family and grandchildren. There's an occasional skirmish but I'm having a "still waters" (Psalm 23:2 NKJV) season. I'm enjoying it as I'm sure God will recruit me for a few more battles before I go home. I'm keeping the armor on.

God has battles being fought on more fronts than I can imagine. It takes self-control to face our fears, inadequacies, desire for comfort and safety, and turn and take a stand when God commissions us. In standing, we breathe fire on the enemy and he will definitely fire back. I would run for the woods if I didn't believe God is bigger than any enemy and will give me His strength, heart, power and armor to fight the good fight.

In my own little circle I have friends who:

- Feed the poor and provide weekend meals for school children.
- Visit prisoners (every Thursday night!)
- Volunteer for hospice.
- Speak out against human trafficking and social injustice.
- Come alongside women facing unplanned pregnancies.

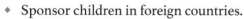
- Sponsor children in foreign countries.
- Advocate for children in the court system.
- Visit and volunteer with the elderly.
- Deliver Meals on Wheels.
- Drive cancer patients to and from their chemotherapy treatments.
- Volunteer as a "big brother" or "big sister" for needy kids.
- Serve as long-term missionaries.
- Tutor school children.
- Provide long-term care for family members.
- Teach with a balance of truth and grace.
- Walk the road of terminal illness with family and friends.
- Overcome addictions and a myriad of other private battles.
- Package supplies for emergency medical teams (and occasionally go with them).
- Maintain homes full of love, laughter, good food, clean clothes, safety and, above all, God.

I'm only scratching the surface of God's work being done in my own little community. God doesn't ask each of us to do all He needs doing. But He asks each of us to do something. Ask the Holy Spirit to fill you with the fruit of self-control when you are faced with the temptation to hide out in your comfort zone. Ask Him to help you take a stand wherever God places you in each season of your life.

Sometimes our battles are highly visible on center stage and sometimes behind the curtain where no one sees. It doesn't matter to God. We may not realize we are fighting battles but every time we perform godly work (or ordinary work in a godly way) we enter the battlefield with God at our side and breathe a little fire on the enemy.

Therefore, my dear brothers, stand firm. Let nothing move you.
Always give yourselves fully to the work of the Lord, because you
know that your labor in the Lord is not in vain.
I Corinthians 15:58

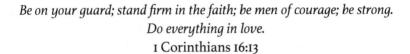

Be on your guard; stand firm in the faith; be men of courage; be strong.
Do everything in love.
1 Corinthians 16:13

 Choices, choices, choices. Submitting to God's will via self-control.

I stared at myself in the full-length mirror in a not very aptly named "fitting" room in Macy's swimwear department. It wasn't an attractive reflection. Apparently I wasn't the only one struggling with the dreaded task of buying a swimsuit. Groans of dismay or bursts of slightly hysterical laughter came from the other dressing rooms. I heard one dear woman say, "Oh, just shoot me!"

I could feel a fit of giggles coming on (similar to the day I got stuck trying on a Spanx) but I needed to make a decision. Out of the seven swimsuits I selected to try, two had made the finals. Both suits were my favorite color, royal blue, and similarly cut. One, however, possessed a "magic tummy-control panel" and the other simply covered me up. I don't know where the magic panel put my tummy but it did make me look a bit slimmer through the middle. Unfortunately, it cost $160.00. The one which covered my tummy but made no attempt to control it cost $55.00. Sadly, neither swimsuit did anything to improve my dimpled thighs, wrinkly cleavage, saggy upper arms or my neck.

I was sorely tempted by the "magic tummy-control panel" which would at least improve one out of five effects of being well on the other side of middle age. To make the decision harder I knew my wallet contained enough cash to buy the non-magical suit. The tummy-controller would have to go on the VISA which would probably tip Rich's teetering budget over the edge. Was the magic panel worth an extra $105.00?

I sat down on the bench to think. If I swam laps every day or took a water aerobics class or was an Olympic diver I could justify an expensive suit. Maybe, two. However, I'm not fond of water-based activities and simply needed a suit in case my grandchildren forced me to go in the pool on our family vacation. I didn't want to pray about my choice because I knew what the Holy Spirit would say. Hmmm. The fact that I was afraid to ask meant I already knew the answer. I felt an unexpected rush of relief as I paid cash for suit number two and headed home. Surprisingly, it looked better at home without the comparison of the magic panel. Rich thought I looked great. As an added bonus, it rained on vacation and I never had to wear it!

You may be wondering what this story has to do with self-control. Well, I'll tell you. My "self" really wanted the suit with the magic panel but I chose to let my decision be controlled by the Holy Spirit. He tends to know what He's doing. This wasn't particularly virtuous on my part as I yielded rather reluctantly, but I made the right decision.

Since this book is about the Fruit of the Spirit, and this section about sharing the fruit of self-control, let's take a look at what my life would possibly look like without God-centered self-control:

- I would love if I felt loving and loved in return.
- I would be joyful if circumstances were going my way.
- I would be at peace if there were no conflicts in my life—nothing to rock my boat.
- I would be patient if everyone behaved as they should and no one crossed me.
- I would be kind if I were in a pleasant mood and not distracted.
- I would be good if it were beneficial to me and didn't demand too much.
- I would be faithful unless faithfulness hurt or became inconvenient.
- I would be gentle with the sweet and innocent but turn a cold shoulder to the unlovely or difficult.
- I would choose self-control if it were to my advantage.

Under God's plan, the Fruit of the Spirit comes in one package. Each quality is bathed in love and is to be exhibited regardless of our feelings or circumstances. Consciously submitting our will to God, minute by minute if necessary, tethers us to the Holy Spirit who gives the strength, holy passion and freedom to live self-controlled, Spirit-led lives.

I wish I could say I have completely submitted my will to God's leading but, of course, I haven't. I still make "me, my and mine" choices. I'm still a sucker for glittery temptations. But I'm beginning to relax and give more and more over to the Spirit. Sometimes it's hard but it's always good. It's very freeing to let go and leave some things behind.

I realize my swimsuit dilemma is a minor event. We frequently face much larger choices and temptations which can significantly impact our lives and the lives of those around us. However, if we can learn to make godly selections in the dressing room we will be better equipped to face the vast array of expensive choices we face out there in the mall.

I believe God began the Fruit of the Spirit with love and ended with self–control for a reason. Love provides the sun, the rain, the nutrients and the fertile soil for the fruit to grow and flourish. Self-control grows deep roots, provides stability and keeps the fruit attached to the branches and the branches attached to the tree. Together they bring in a bountiful harvest for God's people to enjoy and share.

I am the vine; you are the branches. If a man remains in me and I in him,
he will bear much fruit; apart from me you can do nothing.
John 15:5

You did not choose me, but I chose you and appointed you to go
and bear fruit—fruit that will last.
John 15:16

Therefore, since we are surrounded by such a great cloud of witnesses,
let us throw off everything that hinders and the sin that so easily
entangles, and let us run with perseverance the race marked out for us.
Let us fix our eyes on Jesus, the author and perfecter of our faith,
who for the joy set before him endured the cross, scorning its shame,
and sat down at the right hand of the throne of God.
Consider him who endured such opposition from sinful men,
so that you will not grow weary and lose heart.
Hebrews 12:1-3

FRUIT FOR THOUGHT

Self-Control

Nurturing Fruit

1. What is the first thing that comes to mind when you think of "lack of self-control" in your own life? (You don't have to share.)

2. Does reading a chapter from Proverbs every day sound like a profitable exercise for self-control? Try it for a few days and write your thoughts. Did any of the proverbs jump out at you?

3. Do you have any "sneaky rats" in your thought life eating away at your self-control? How could you cooperate with God to help you jettison these thoughts?

4. What areas of your life could use a dose of moderation? What aspects of our culture cause discontent and make self-control difficult? Where is your treasure?

5. What is a temptation that overwhelms your self-control and sweeps you into the "impact zone?"

6. Is your armor hanging in the closet? Are you putting it on before heading into your day? (Idea: tape a note in your closet or on the bathroom mirror with Ephesians 6:10-17 written out. Read carefully before dressing).

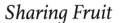

Sharing Fruit

1. Can you visualize a self-control filter being inserted in your head (a bit uncomfortable at first but basically painless). What would end up as pulp to be tossed and what would the Holy Spirit allow through? How would this impact others?

2. Have you ever allowed lack of self-control to create a problem that didn't need creating? What happened and how did others react?

3. Has anyone been a stumbling block in your Christian walk? (You don't have to name names!) How did you react? Have you ever been the stumbling block? If you became a Christian later in life, what people or situations frustrated or encouraged your journey to the cross? List three ways you can encourage others in their Christian walk.

4. Has God called you to "take a stand" (big or small) in the past? Is He calling you now to "breathe a little fire on the enemy?"

5. What would (or does) your life look like without God-centered, self-control? How does your lack of self-control affect others? Which of the three verses at the end of #5 "Choices, Choices, Choices" is the most encouraging? Why?

❄ ❄ ❄

Grab your notebook and write out...

❖ One Scripture from this chapter that is particularly meaningful to you.

❖ Your Thoughts and Stories

❄ ❄ ❄

EPILOGUE

Today is December 31ˢᵗ. New Year's Eve. A perfect day for writing the final pages of a book. I should have finished last December but life got complicated and messy. I suspect God wanted it that way. He wanted me to stumble, get lost, feel like a fraud and tell Him I simply couldn't finish this book. I think He wanted me to see "fruit flies" up close and personal. Discouragement, depression, frustration, inadequacy, fear, anxiety, feeling unequal to the task—I faced a swarm of spiritual fruit flies.

God didn't scold me or accuse me. He simply took me to Deuteronomy. He used Moses words as he spoke to Joshua in preparation for entering the Promised Land to remind me He was with me and could take out any fruit fly that threatened His plan for me.

Be strong and courageous.
Do not be afraid or terrified because of them,
for the LORD your God goes with you;
he will never leave you nor forsake you.
Deuteronomy 31:6

The LORD himself goes before you and will be with you;
he will never leave you nor forsake you.
Do not be afraid; do not be discouraged.
Deuteronomy 31:8

God is so good and I love Him so. He knows if I knew what He expected right from the start I would freeze like a deer in the headlights and get run over by my own doubt and fear. Every step of my Christian walk He has held my hand and, when He deemed me ready, we turned a corner, then another and another.

I am such a slow learner. Preparation for writing and learning about the Fruit of the Spirit were essential first steps. Then we reached a corner and God guided me into the pages of this book. Now that it's done, I thought we'd reached our destination. But wait—He still holds my hand and, in what I suspect to be a rather gleeful way, is leading me around another bend onto a road lined with fruit-laden trees.

God never meant for this journey to end. By His "goodness and love," He intends it to continue "...all the days of my life..." (Psalm 23:6). I have my overflowing basket of fruit and you have yours. The Holy Spirit will keep us endlessly supplied with fresh, delicious fruit as long as we keep giving it away.

He will make it happen.

Now to Him who is able to do exceeding abundantly beyond all that we
ask or think, according to the power that works within us,
to Him be the glory in the church and in Christ Jesus
to all generations forever and ever.
Amen.
Ephesians 3:20-21 (NASB)

Between You and Me

Bless your heart for reading all my stories and taking this journey with me. Along the way, God taught me so much about my spiritual fruit flies and His will for my life. He encouraged me with the knowledge that change is a life-long process.

We've come a long way together and now I would like to read your stories. The stories God is using to open your mind and heart to the Fruit of the Spirit. Please send me an e-mail and let me know how the Spirit is teaching you to bear fruit in your life. Thank you.

yourstories@tangiblefaithpublishing.com

CPSIA information can be obtained
at www.ICGtesting.com
Printed in the USA
FFHW01n0010041018
48656993-52646FF

9 781732 240308